Jesus Bootlegged

Jesus Bootlegged

George Elerick

BOOKS

Winchester, UK
Washington, USA

First published by O-Books, 2011
O Books is an imprint of John Hunt Publishing Ltd., The Bothy, Deershot Lodge, Park Lane, Ropley,
Hants, SO24 0BE, UK
office1@o-books.net
www.o-books.com

For distributor details and how to order please visit the 'Ordering' section on our website.

Text copyright: George Elerick 2010

ISBN: 978 1 84694 510 6

A CIP catalogue record for this book is available from the British Library.

Design: Tom Davies

Printed in the UK by CPI Antony Rowe
Printed in the USA by Offset Paperback Mfrs, Inc

We operate a distinctive and ethical publishing philosophy in all
areas of its business, from its global network of authors to
production and worldwide distribution.

CONTENTS

The popular Protestant piety of yesteryear no longer speaks to tens of millions of people who have yet found nothing to replace it. The church that has institutionalized those beliefs is crumbling. Elerick hopes that Jesus can survive, and that, stripped of projections and accretions, and described in the language of today, he can call together new communities of disciples. May he be right, and may this book, written for confused and disillusioned youth and adults, further this needed transformation.

John Cobb Professor Emeritus, Claremont School of Theology

George Elerick has an invitation for you in Jesus Bootlegged. It is an invitation to think smartly, talk honestly, and live faithfully. Jesus Bootlegged is a faith classic for those in emerging culture. For those looking for a conversation partner who is not satisfied with the same old answers, George Elerick's Jesus Bootlegged is great place to start.

Doug Pagitt, Pastor Solomon's Porch - Minneapolis, JoPa Productions Owner, Author of *Church in the Inventive Age*

This is an excellent example of the honest and truly helpful reading of Jesus that is emerging in our time. At last we have rescued Jesus from seminaries with their pre-determined and safe conclusions. Read, and be consoled, challenged, and inspired all at the same time!

[Fr.] Richard Rohr, O.F.M., Center for Action and Contemplation, Albuquerque, New Mexico

Not since the Reformation has the institutional church faced challenges like those of today -- and the pace of change is only increasing. George Elerick points us in exactly the right direction: back to the movement of that startling 1st-century rabbi, Jesus. Here is a guide for those who are ready to deconstruct Christendom and "rethink everything" for the saké of the gospel... a courageous call to radical discipleship!

Philip Clayton, Author of *Transforming Christian Theology*

George Elerick has produced a serious sassy sizzling heartfelt and learned reconstitution of Jesus that will repay the attention of anyone who is not afraid to think outside the lines and speak about Jesus in terms of ordinary life. His book is written in an engaging way that draws from deep wells and deserves a wide hearing.

John Caputo, Thomas J Watson Professor of Religion and Humanities and Professor of Philosophy, Syracuse University, New York

Acknowledgements:

Thanks to those who gave up their couches, coffee mugs, and bleeding ears to get me to this point. Thanks to friends, family and enemies for believing in me. This is dedicated to my beautiful wife Deborah who believed this was possible, the Bridgers, the Wilsons, the Bubbs, the Corks and so many more, they know who they are. This is for all of you.

Introduction

meet the author.

I used to think that life was about having all the answers. That it was about arriving. In fact, a large portion of my teen years and 20s was spent trying to find answers. My childhood was varied in terms of religious exposure. I was baptised into the Catholic Church as an infant. I then went to a non-denominational church. My adopted mom thought it would be good for my siblings and I to be exposed to other expressions of faith, so my mother invited in-house lessons from the Jehovah's Witnesses and teachers from the Church of Jesus Christ of Latter Day Saints. This spirit of tolerance has carried with me, although, there was a period where I thought Christianity had all the answers, I am not so sure what we have now is what was always meant to be. I used to read the Bible like it somehow had the magic words for every moment I was ever going to have. I thought it was this collection of quotes that would heal all of my teenage angst. For me now, it has become something more, something that is less about answers and more about the narrative I am invited into. But, its not a narrative for the faint at heart, it calls us to leave things behind that we might think are important. Some writers went so far as to say that our under-standings of God were the enemy. One of the things that keeps me coming back to this holy book is that authors found the divine within the contradictions. They even write about the frustration of trying to find God in these contradicting moments. And we get front row seats. The more I read the scriptures, the more I find my story unfolding, along with all the contradictions, and I try to find God in them. So, in this book, I too might contradict myself, and for me, that's okay, because the Jews believed contradiction made life beautiful. For example, I might talk about how being saved (in traditional theology) means something, and in other places, how getting saved (within context) might mean something completely different yet use them separately as if they both are right. Or how I have hope for the church and in another moment I might say we need something better. Some might say this is irresponsible scholarship, but how can it be irresponsible if contradictions for me are a necessary part of the discovery? We need contradiction to bring the peace we so crave. It's these paradoxes that the ancient Jewish writers were so comfortable with. This might not be a comfortable book to read, I get that. I invite you to challenge this book, add to the conversation, burn it or engage with it. This book isn't about providing solid answers, this isn't a manual on how to get it right. This isn't a fool-proof scheme on how to follow a step-by-step guide on how to live life with God. I wish it were that easy at times, but it isn't and that is what intrigues me and drives me to ask more questions, not because I am looking for a systematic approach to God, but because curiosity leads me by the nose to find the God that is beyond my theology. To be honest, I am not fully comfortable with everything I have written in here, but its part of my journey, its part of where I am at and thought it would be valuable to this ongoing dialogue. I need to be honest because this is where I am at, and being vulnerable is part of the process of deciding what I need to shed and where that deconstruction might lead me. So, this is less about the answers and more about the journey we are embarking on together. At one point my worldview would have been more about us working together to hammer it all down. If 'answers' were a person and had breath, I would be exhaling what he was inhaling. It was all about the pursuit. It still is. It's just not about the answers anymore. It's about the adventure. It's about the scandalous recognition that I am no longer sinful but still need Jesus to show me everything. It's about learning to embrace my darkness and light and allowing the light enough space to save me. It's about walking down the street and realizing that no matter how many fences I erect, we are all connected. It's about being okay that I don't have all the answers, which makes life more about the journey. The journey is the destination as the cliché says. Life then becomes this experience that invites us to be the child we were meant to be who chases innocently after the mystery. This approach allows for us then to not be as concerned about whether the Bible is inerrant, but it allows more space to discover the purpose of it and how it and any other book can help change us to into better followers in the way of Jesus. It becomes less about marketing and more about becoming a maven of life. This book also tries to put some of the new thoughts in the Emergent Conversation on God, Jesus and others into accessible language for those who are new to the person and message of Jesus or who want another way to see what they already know. I would say that, none of us have it nailed down. We haven't arrived. This book hasn't arrived. I don't know if its about an arrival at all. Because that would assume that there is an in and out club to be a part of. So the book invites people to let go of a dualistic way of thinking, and become more aware that God pulls this whole thing together. It is about being broken and fixed and in jaw-dropping awe of what truth, Christianity, Buddha, Jesus, Ghandi, Martin Luther King jr, gays, straights, atheists, Bono, Mother Teresa, St. John of the cross, sunrises, sunsets, rivers, oceans, pain, laughter, music and tears still yet have to teach me.

meet bob.
Bob is a 50-year old friend of mine who is dying of emphysema. He still likes to smoke and he kindly offers me one every time. He lives in low-income housing with his next-door neighbour who is trying to get off of heroin. Bob and I met when I was doing some youth work and experimenting with how far is too far in getting teenagers to interact with those they might never think to have a conversation with. Bob told me one day, while

walking through town, how he had never met a good Christian. Ever. A few months later after making friends with his neighbour and cleaning his apartment, Bob texted me and said "I have never met Christians like you before!" Which was an incredibly giving statement. Bob had grown up in the church, I think he thought God left him when his wife and daughter left him. See, Bob had this worldview that those in Christianity were stale and judgemental, but the simple act of teenagers cleaning his friend's apartment was enough to change everything. It was a small gesture that had infinite lasting effects. The hope for this book is that it is part of a small gesture in a wider conversation that has been going on since the first star emerged in the sky. My hope is to spark even more conversation about who the person of Jesus is and how he challenges us to be a people who go out and change economies, societies, churches, theologies and each other in the name of redemptive grace, love, and restoration.

meet jesus.
Jesus spoke Aramaic. The scriptures we now have were translated from the Aramaic into the Greek. The authors, whoever they were, had an audience they were trying to reach. Their desire was to get the message of Jesus out into the world to as many people as possible. It just so happens that the "ends of the earth" that Jesus instructed them to go to happened to be predominantly Greek speaking peoples and so this framed their apparent need to translate their scripture into relevant documents that spoke to the readers. It would have been much like the missionaries today who have translated scripture into relevant dialects to give out Bibles to the people groups they are serving with and among. Some people think this might be tampering with authority or validity of scripture, and yet they are okay with missionaries completely translating it into another language? So, where is the plumbline, and who gets to determine it? One thing we can't get away from is that Jesus did speak a specific language and lived

with a certain geographical place in history that adhered to certain customs and practices. When we read scripture from the Hebrew/Aramaic sometimes we get a completely different rendering and sometimes a completely new message that we might have never discovered unless we dive deeper into the culture, language and life of Jesus. The intention here is not to demonize the orthodox message of Christianity, but rather to add to the ongoing conversation of who Jesus is. There will be moments I will share my heart on some of the theological percep-tions that have been so misconstrued that their interpretations have done the exact opposite of what those verses were talking about. Having said all this, I try to approach the scripture with the assumptions of a theopoetic practitioner, which is to say that there isn't one objective interpretation, but that there are many that reflect all the possibilities that the message might entail. It is also important to recognize that the authors are writing in hindsight and also are projecting their views of God into their writing. In this sense, they have a particular agenda in mind. I will leave it to you to discover what those are. This doesn't change whether the Bible has value or not, but it does allow us to rediscover God on his terms. To discover a God who is committed to the world he created so much so that he partners with his creation to find ways to repair the divine within it. I am just not all that comfortable with a god who confesses a religion about himself. Or a god who says I have to sign-up to a certain amount of confessions or have to go to church so many times. As significant as these things might be, I just can't see that kind of God anywhere in the scriptures. I do see a God who believes in every one of us. The Jewish understanding of God is that He is the only divine being who has an immensely high view of His creation. Christianity is child of Judaism, and somewhere along the way Christianity adopted the worldview that mankind is incapable of transcending himself, sin, issues and anything else that could fit in this category. The ancient Jewish followers of

5

God would disagree. Their view is that God created us because He believes in us and our ability to make the world a beautiful place for everyone to experience. This book is about finding Jesus through all of the rubble that certain presumptions within Christianity have led those who follow after him to believe which aren't true, but to also introduce a Jesus who wasn't here to start a club but to revolutionize the world and everyone in it. This book is about trying to restore the implications behind an all-inclusive message of the peasant teacher from Nazareth who spoke Aramaic.

Some might assume that changing the language of scripture effects either the authority or inspiration of its pages. This would be like saying that learning a new language strips the power of the message from its context. But this is not so. If we can agree that Jesus spoke Aramaic, then recapturing his message from his language would not only be considered proper stewardship of linguistics but it would also allow us to get a panoramic view of the intention of his message. It restores the context rather than creating another, which is what happens when we read scripture solely from the Greek. Some might be more comfortable with a comparative linguistic approach. The only problem is that again Greek would strip Jesus of His Aramaic context. I think it would be helpful in our approach to understand Jesus in context, to adopt the precept of cognitive linguistics, which asserts our brains don't understand words automatically. That their meanings have to be learned. That the process of understanding is done over time. And maybe this needs to be the case with journey towards a transformational kind of Christianity as well. But that process of rediscovery means we need to let go of some things.

I am taking more of a post-modern approach to historical linguistics that seeks to restore Jesus in a world that He knew, loved and wanted to redeem. When we do this then we can come to see that the words of Jesus were intentionally inclusive to even those who opposed his ideas. It was a message that God could have initially chosen anyone to carry. It just so happens that when we join the story, the Jews happened to be chosen by Yahweh to carry his message to the rest of the known world. They focused so much on the fact that they were chosen that they lost out on the opportunity to transform the world. And if we focus all our energies on what is right and who is wrong then we too become part of our own history of people who sat and did nothing for a world in crisis, which essentially is at the heart of the gospel message of Jesus Christ of Nazareth. So this is an invitation to wake up and see that we have been given a message that can transform lives, and that to keep this message to ourselves is to essentially agree to irresponsibility and laziness. If we choose the opposite and carry this message (embedded with global implications) in defiant hope that love can change everything than not only can we experience personal transformation we can see it happen right before our very eyes.

Jesus Bootlegged

Believe those who are seeking the truth; doubt those who find it. —
Andre Gide

Our family used to go camping a lot. I think when I entered the
world, I must have arrived with tent pegs in my hand. I've
always loved the outdoors. As a child, I used to explore the green
forests, the dirty paths and the blue skies at a place called Crystal
Lake. I still think about the days when we used to drink directly
from the lake, and it was so clear it was like looking in a mirror.
One of the habits I have picked up from my camping days has
almost turned into an honest obsession. You see, I collect stars. I
try my hardest to spend a lot of time underneath them. It's like a
sort of tapestry that invites me in. It feels as if we are long lost
lovers. Somehow when I sit underneath them, the world comes
together and it all makes sense. But what if there's more to these
stars? Maybe the stars, as beautiful and unfolding as they are,
are part of a larger narrative, a bigger story. And this story is still
happening, in fact, you and I are part of it. If we draw the curtain
and peer behind the stars we might see that there is more. Could
this be the same for the message of Jesus?[1]

peering behind the stars.
Most of the world is familiar with Jesus. At least the Christian
Jesus that is. What about the Jewish Jesus? Is He really that
different? What if our discoveries of the Jewish Jesus force us to
re-evaluate our affiliations with Christianity? What if what we
find out about this Jesus requires us to let go of certain presumptions about the Jesus we thought we always knew? This first
chapter is all about meeting Jesus for the first time again. Jesus
was a peripatetic Jewish teacher who lived over 2,000 years ago.
He lived in what is now modern day Palestine. He possibly grew

up in a town called Nazareth that is still around today. Some
scholars even say he might have been born in Nazareth rather
than Bethlehem. The center of any Jewish town was the market-
place and local shops. It was the ultimate mall where everyone
came to sip on lattes and talk about the latest fashions of the day.
It would have had the same vibe as a bar or pub. It was the local
centre for gossip, philosophy and theology. According to *Jesus
Central* it was a place where "local merchants would sell sacrificial animals at excessive cost in order to turn a profit from the
tourists or religious seekers that would come to the temple." The
Jews lived in isolated insular-type communities where people
would experience life together in every way. Individual decisions
were made as a community, raising your children was a
communal practice which is very different to most cultures today.
Most houses were 1-2 bedrooms and they had dirt floors, not the
place for a vacuum! Jesus was a travelling teacher who was recog-
nized as a Rabbi by those who followed after Him. The title of
Rabbi was a Hebrew word that simply meant teacher. But in their
time and history, Rabbi's were more like rockstars. You wanted to
be just like a Rabbi. Jesus had this particular message that was
referred to by most of his followers as the gospel. Some modern
followers of Jesus believe the gospel is defined by a single prayer
wherein the person saying the words admits that they are sinners
and that they need God. So what's the story behind the story
then? Well, the word gospel in the first-century was a word that
the Roman Emperors would use to describe their political
agendas. Julius Caesar would have called his political dreams for
Rome his gospel. Jesus steps onto the scene and essentially
redefines what the word gospel means in light of his transformational message. At this point, the term re-emerged as something
more than just political vernacular, and it started igniting this
new reality that Jesus believed all men could experience in the
here and now. Maybe Jesus still believes that now. This new
gospel looks different for each person, because we all experience

different circumstances. It isn't a mandated gospel that people need to be a part of. It isn't a religion for the few. Once we begin to define the message of Jesus as a message for an elite group of people, it becomes nothing more than an event you go to once a week. For example, the person who can't seem to pay their bills or buy groceries for their hungry children, part of the gospel for them would mean that they could come to a place of personal sustainability. The gospel speaks into the lives and situations of people. Somehow though, through centuries and centuries of history and narrow interpretation, the message of Jesus has been distorted. Maybe a better word might be stolen or hijacked[3]. Mostly hijacked from within. This chapter is going to set the ground work for those who might be interested in the on-going conversation amongst Christians. It is also an invitation to follow me, engage with me, and find the real message of Jesus for the world and what may have happened to it.

Typically, Jesus is the mascot for Christianity, an institutional religion that has become more than it should be and less than it could be. Some people use the history of this movement as a plumb-line for how we are doing now, but I think that's where most of the problem lies, that was then and this is now. Maybe what we need is to be evangelized by the Christianity of the future rather than being coddled by Christianity of the past. This isn't to say that there isn't any good in what has been offered, but if spend all of our time focusing on the Christianity then we will never have a chance to see what it could look like now. Unfortunately, the Christianity of the past along the way has morphed into an institution. A system. A regime. An empire. I think its also important to realize that Jesus wasn't a Christian. To make Jesus the supposed icon of one religious tradition is to unknowingly take a message with universal significance and make it small. It would be implying that Jesus is the prisoner of orthodoxy, tenets and dogma. If Jesus is bigger than a religion, than he himself cannot be captive of any one of them. I just can't

see Jesus standing in a church waving a flag that has Baptist, Methodist, Mormon, or Buddhist on it. I see Jesus whispering in the lives of those above and inviting them into a new way of life. Inviting them to serve one another, love another, heal one another and make the world a better place. I just can't sign on to the view that God is a cheerleader for a set of beliefs that humans have to follow, but I can support a God who believes that all of humanity has what it takes to follow in his footsteps. Where is that God? Where has he gone? The pages of the Bible paint a picture of men, women and children who followed a person not an institution.

choosing anyone.

The scene opens up on a nearby hill where Jesus used to play as a boy. Jesus is getting ready to give his first recorded sermon. This hill would have brought back so many interesting memories for Jesus. According to the Catholic Encyclopedia [4]"...the scene of this discourse is traditionally located on Karn Hattin (or Kurun Hattîn), the Horns of Hattin, a mountain which derives its name from the little village at its northern base and from the two cones or horns which crown its summit. Karn Hattin is in Galilee, an easy distance from Nazareth, Cana, and Mt. Tabor to the southwest, of Tiberias and Lake Gennesaret (the Sea of Galilee) to the east, and of Capharnaum (Capernaum) to the northeast, in the centre, therefore, of much of the ministry of Jesus." He and his dad would have been to the city nearby quite a bit to do some construction work and probably made some lifelong friends there. His audience would have most likely known who he was. As Jesus is sitting there with some of his close friends and followers, he begins talking with them about a simpler time. And the act of reminiscing, brings him to this sort of dreaming outloud—a new kind of society. In the time of Jesus, the Jewish people were in national disarray. They were under the iron hand of Rome, that would kill people on a whim if citizens didn't conform. Romans would dismember people and put their heads on a stake and place those stakes on the roads that led out of the occupied cities. This would be a reminder to citizens and enemies that no-one crosses Rome for any reason. This is the setting for Jesus' message of liberation and hope. One of the nearby shepherds listens in and picks up on some everyday Jewish language. He, as a Jew, would have understood what Jesus was saying. But it's said in such a fresh way, that he rushes to gather some of his friends and some random pedestrians and they start to listen in to this new Rabbi who has just come on the scene. Sometimes all we need to spark hope and ignite faith is to hear an old word said in a new way. The way Jesus speaks is like nothing they've ever heard before. He begins to speak of a society where the poor are the richest, and where the hungry are the filled. These words begin turning an identity-less people and their way of life upside down. You see when Jesus is talking to this group of people he isn't dreaming of some kind of distant utopia somewhere out there, he is envisioning something that is possible now and he is inviting them to dream with Him. A world where people look at each other as equals, where enemies are loved and women are full of value and children have something to say. This unassuming Rabbi was attempting to re-create a world of unlimited possibilities, not simply an exclusive community with limited possibilities. People like Martin Luther King Jr., Desmond Tutu and Mother Teresa caught on to this reality and have found ways to implement it in our world today. Without knowing it, they were being Jesus, not simply his followers. Jesus' audience would have included prostitutes, shepherds, the sick, the poor and the needy. And he has this group of outcasts stuck together in the same room. He gave them words entangled with a defiant hope with the belief that they could rise above their current status and circumstance. He does the same with us.

the unclean ones.

You can just see it. For years and years, many of these people have been told they don't matter to anyone or anything. Either by the Roman government or the document they called the Law. Imagine the gravity of his words falling on hungry ears. They've been told they don't have value and they have learned to believe that the lie is true. What lies have we come to believe about ourselves that aren't true? Maybe someone else's words, or views or their version of the 'law' has somehow left us empty and scarred like the Mosaic Law did to some of those on the fringe. Now this law was aptly named the Mosaic Law because it was an ancient list of expectations from the divine given to the Jewish prophet Moses thousands of years before Jesus came on the scene. It was an over-informed code of conduct that everyone was expected to live by. Most Jews today refer to it as *halakha* which is Hebrew for the "way of walking [5]". It draws this picture of life as this dusty path we all get to journey on, that to follow God was to walk with Him, and for them this is how they walked. Now, some of the Jews thought that all 613 rules of this Mosaic Law had to be followed word for word or you would be condemned by God. If for some reason you couldn't follow the rules or didn't want to, the community would ostracize you. Pick on you and then force you to live on the street begging for food and love. If you were born with a deformity, you were dirty. You were already an outcast before you had the choice. For some of these people, their families and status in the community had been literally stripped from them. These people were nicknamed the "unclean ones"; their sickness and their moral laws separated them from their close friends and from any future within their society. There were many more that seemed never to just fit comfortably into a niche within their culture, much like many today, so what do you do with what you don't know? Well, you reject it, of course. They were the rejected ones. They were kicked to the curb. They sat outside the city gates and hoped for a new kind of hope to believe in. And Jesus was there to give it to them. Maybe the gospel we have and the gospel that was—are worlds apart. And this is what the post-modern conversation is all about, trying to recapture the gospel that was meant to be. If we take a closer look, we will see that Jesus strategically chose those who the world might naturally have rejected.

followers.

Let's take a deeper look at those who followed Jesus, so we can get a better idea of just how "outside" his followers were. Luke was a Gentile doctor. A practical healer. People would have visited him for medical help. It would be too easy to overlook what a Gentile was and simply label him an outsider. A Gentile was also outside the religious sect, not just a denominational difference...he would have been more like a modern-day buddhist or maybe what we might more closely consider as a Native American healer. And Jesus entrusted the Kingdom [6] to him.

Also Mary Magdalene, who also might of been one of the financiers of Jesus ministry, was a woman who dealt with her demons. According to the story, she might have been possessed up to 7 different times. She still struggled with her demons after meeting Jesus. But the Rabbi saw something valuable in his disciple. So Jesus' ministry was sustained by a demoniac. And by a woman, and women in that society simply had no value. And Jesus supported her by believing she had what it took to build the Kingdom of God on earth.

Then we meet up with a guy named Matthew. A tax-collector. Now, try to imagine a tax-collector who randomly shows up on your doorstep for a routine surprise audit. All those feelings that are coursing through your veins right now would have been felt by most Jewish people, plus a side-order of betrayal. Jewish tax-collectors were known as double-crossers. They worked for the enemy—Rome. The collectors not only collected taxes from their own people, but they would also overcharge each person pocket the difference. And for the most part, the price was ludicrously outrageous. This act alone helped create another set of helpless people on the fringe, the homeless[7]. This was Matthew. A betrayer.

Judas was most likely a member of a band of people called the Sicarii [8]. The Sicarii were a bunch of extreme nationalists who believed that the only good Roman was a dead Roman. Not to mention that Judas was also the one in line to betray his friend Jesus for some money. So, Judas would have been a terrorist, a mercenary of sorts, who according to our story would have only been looking out for number one. And yep, you guessed it, Jesus chose him too [9].

A mystic healer. A prostitute. A political thief. A terrorist. And this is just getting started. This is who Jesus chose to build His Kingdom with. This is still who he chooses to build his Kingdom with even now.

Liberating Christianity

All religions, arts and sciences are branches of the same tree. All these aspirations are directed toward ennobling man's life, lifting it from the sphere of mere physical existence and leading the individual towards freedom. - Albert Einstein

My mother was a prostitute. She would sneak away in the middle of the night while my sisters and I were fast asleep, dreaming of ways to keep our innocence alive. We were a very poor family. She was only doing what she needed to, to help put food on the table. In fact, both of my parents found other ways to try and put clothes in our drawers and dreams in our heads. Together, they sold and did every drug under the sun to pay for bills so we could enjoy things like milk, cereal, and electricity. At least that's what I've been told. As a four-year old you don't really question what is going on around you because the world is a beautiful and intriguing place to be in. Between the conversations I have had with my two sisters, adopted mother and a de-contextualized reading of some notes of my custody battles, I have created an inherited hybrid version of my childhood that might not be true. I am still learning things that might be old in the scheme of history but are rather new to me. I think this is what's happening within Christianity, there are some people who aren't necessarily sure that what is inherited about our faith is all that there is. Naturally, if someone has questions about who they are, where they've come from and how they got to where they are then they want to find ways to discover that information. I am one such person. I want to find the details of my childhood so I can make sense of who I am, not that I can't do that without the information, but it sure does help! Asking questions can be scary, because it might lead you out of your current sphere of knowledge and introduce into details that you may not really want to know. For example, some might wonder why there is so much unnecessary tension in the climate of the Church because it seems some people might have accepted their inherited theism without question and don't want to know what's on the other side. Their habits of not knowing have become a ritual. Like philosopher Frederich Nietzsche once said "We still do not yet know where the drive for truth comes from. For so far we have heard only of the duty which society imposes in order to exist: to be truthful means to employ the usual metaphors. Thus, to express it morally, this is the duty to lie according to a fixed convention, to lie with the herd and in a manner binding upon everyone. Now man of course forgets that this is the way things stand for him. Thus he lies in the manner indicated, unconsciously and in accordance with habits which are centuries' old; and precisely by means of this unconsciousness and forgetfulness he arrives at his sense of truth."

I think what's happened is the Church has learned to accept the usual metaphors as the only possible truth. I think mostly out of fear, out of a habit of fear. If someone offers a different view outside of the inherited faith, than they are labeled as a heretic, Satan or something much worse. The religion of Christianity has become a habitual practice rather than a way of life. It has become a gnostic faith rather than a mystic faith. It is now become a failed gospel that has been birthed out of the Enlightenment and forced into a scientific mold of presuppositional statements that are forced to end there. It has become a religion of comfort rather than a religion of question. Questions start the journey, answers stop it. If truth is unfolding and itself progresses than we have to chase after it, rather than try to find ways to colonize what we're not comfortable with. So how did we get this way?

I think the God-like character of Christof in the movie *The Truman Show* has a possible answer, the movie is about a man who grows up in a world fabricated by a movies studio who airs his life to listening viewers. Truman is the main character who struggles with the world around him and begins to question his existence and if the world around him is even real. This line of questioning sets in motion the rest of those who were casted to be his friends and family to prevent him from finding the significant answers to his questions because if he does find what he's looking for it will not only be the end of his world as he knows, it will be the end of the show. One of the shows producers asks Christof why it took so long for Truman to begin questioning the world around him and Christ of responds "We accept the reality of the world with which we are presented, it's as simple as that."

The reality is that we have accepted thousands of years of interpretation and have called it truth and have treated it as 'gospel. We have presented a Christianity to the world that has become monolithic and innately digressive. We have perpetuated the lie that following in the Way of Jesus means one must easily accept a certain amount of communal truth and never question it. We've gotten to comfortable with our fear of change. This isn't to say that what has been offered for all these years is wrong; it just means we can't accept it any longer as the only truth about God out there. Some of the reason why we don't know what's out there is because for millennia the church was the monarchy. It was the media, the police, the rulers and the preachers. The church at one time owned all things informational. I think it was a mix of both. I think we have gotten comfortable with truth that's been tamed. A truth that has been watered down and manageable. It might even go deeper even into our neo-cortexes.

According to the Brain Works Project[10], an initiative that seeks to understand how we learn, why we learn, and how those discoveries can empower parents to better raise their children say this: "Our brain struggles to understand new or strange experiences or information. We also know that once we develop a thinking habit, or form beliefs about ourselves or others, it may be difficult to change them. Imagine our thinking brain's crevices and wrinkles being hills and river valleys. The river valleys, where we store past experiences, go deeper into our brain the more water (experiences) that runs through them. Once a river of thought and behavior carves a deep course in our brain system of neurons, that river will continue to run along that same deep path whenever we have similar experiences! Now consider how difficult it is for us to change that deep and powerful river's path. Making that adjustment takes a lot of work." Maybe the reason why its so difficult to abandon what we've been taught that might not be true is because we have created shortcuts in our brain (the brains way of being lazy and irresponsible) that have allowed us to embrace the illusion that what was and is, is all there ever could be. Yet, if we choose to accept that as a reality than we too join in on the irresponsibility of the processes of brain. The more we choose to become victims of our ignorance the more we discover the God we want to discover rather than the God that is.

And the more we perpetuate things like this, the more inevitable the death of Christianity becomes a reality. This is why we need a new word. This isn't a new word that is the new objective view of Jesus, Scripture and God. It is one that celebrates the diversity and otherness of the Creator of all mankind. The word Christian doesn't seem to do that anymore. The word that was used in the ancient world by those who didn't follow Jesus and were making fun of those who did was the word Christianos. The word 'ianos' in ancient Greek means to be a 'slave of' to whatever it was compounded with. It was a derogatory term, one filled with anger and disdain. Now the author and missionary Paul spent a lot of time turning himself into a slave of Christ to demonstrate the tenacious spirit of those who chose to follow after Christ and to respond to such a label with hope rather than anger. Paul was trying to redeem a cuss-word and use it for good. But in our world where slavery isn't acceptable, maybe we need something a bit more relevant.

Something like 'imitators of God', or 'followers of the way', or 'Jesus imitators' or maybe even 'God-followers'. These aren't necessarily outside the scope of conventional Christianity and that's okay because not all of what Western Christianity offers is all bad. But we also have to be realistic about the time and place and era of history that we live in. A lot has changed since Paul catalyzed the movement of Christianity and to realize that we might need something a bit more updated isn't being cavalier with our inheritance it is being a good steward of it. This good stewardship leads us also to question the Jesus who hides behind thousands of years of canonized assumptions. If the Jesus we have now clearly isn't the Jesus who was, then we have to keep digging, asking and probing until we find Him. We can start by giving up our sign-on-the-dotted-line approach to the person of Jesus. We can begin by letting go of our facades of Jesus.

jesus of the facade.
Inter-subjectivity is a psycho-analytic practice that states there is a relationship between objects that agree or disagree with one another. That hidden in the tension of the opposing viewpoints is a new birth waiting to arrive on the scene. The theory behind inter-subjectivity is that it invites people to recognize that even if something/someone is disproving the other, the act of disproving the other actually proves its existence. Let's use Christianity as an example. If we spend all of our energy defending Christianity, inter-subjectivity would say that without even being aware of it, we actually disprove it. It's like an atheist overstating their passionate disbelief in the divine and in the disbelief end up demonstrating a God who lives and breathes. Or the person who expends so much energy on over-verbalizing their belief in God ends up being the person who gives up on anything divine. So maybe the only way to find God is to lose Him. Like light and dark, being two sides of the same coin, the same holds true of belief and disbelief. Maybe what we need to

deny are the systematic approaches to Christianity that unintentionally seek to reduce the divine down to a system. When we do this we might be able to find what was meant to be. Maybe we can band together and dig through the rubble of opinionated doctrine and see if we can find Jesus buried in the aftermath of our religious wake. Sometimes we need to come to a place in our faith where we depend less on the creeds and more on God. Where we become more agnostic to religion and more open to understanding the Divine on its own terms. The more we assert our beliefs by utilizing tyrannical methodologies to promote the message of Jesus, the more the methodologies become the very pessimistic rejection we spend our time running from. I am specifically referring to this idea in the Church where people think they need to be conversion consumerists with a shot-gun loaded with Jesus bullets. Conversion was something that the Roman empire imposed upon people in their *Pax Romana* campaign. Rome forced people to believe the way they thought or they had to die. Sometimes people think it's our responsibility to convert others, its not. Love changes everything, not us. We might have to give up control here too. We might have to be peel back the layers of church history that have somehow imprisoned the historical Jesus. One thing is for sure, we need to rescue him, but the rescue may cause you your life. Well, at least the life you have been taught to live. Let's find an escape route!

The *felt* Jesus who would occasionally fall off the Sunday school teachers black tattered board isn't real. That Jesus never existed. Those Jesus' just don't ring true to the person who has lived and breathed God, the person who spent time talking with the outsider people of his day. And we have to be okay with the ambiguity of not knowing everything about who Jesus was. Jesus is intrinsically primary to our developing narratives, but when God made you, I don't think he intended to make another Jesus. However, the person of Jesus is still critical to our understanding of who God is, what God is committed to and how we can partner with God. Jesus is distinctively important for our understanding of how to be people who are personally developed by his thoughts, words, and actions. But if God intended to make little Jesus' everywhere, then Abraham, Moses, Gideon, David and some of the other ancient earth walkers wouldn't have ever lived. God made you to be you. And Jesus introduces this truth as something that is meant for everyone. And this is one of the many things we can take with us on our journey of discovering who God has meant us to be.

What would Jesus' message modernized sound like?

If we were to modernize Christ's message, it would be something like this: "I am here to enable and empower prostitutes, drug dealers, thieves, Buddhists, and anyone else who wants to join this Kingdom movement, to let them know that they have what it takes to live out this new kind of gospel in the here and now."

undefining everything.

I think, far too often in certain Christian huddles there is this need to define people. He's the "pastor's son". She's married to an "ex-drug dealer". He's the son of that "poor family down the road". The whispers haunt us. They single us out and take away all hope of acceptance. Those Christians like to define who's in and who's out. Sometimes within those huddles, there is even this diametric worldview towards mankind, which without even being fully aware of it, supports something more akin to a religious apartheid, rather than anything near the culture of Jesus. Diametrics create a reality where one has to be good and the other has to be bad. For example, she who attends weekly church services is a good person and he who doesn't is a bad person. Or, it's been months since I have stepped into a church. And I am fine with that, not because I don't think I need church but because if I am honest, the church as is – is failing. We were meant for so much more than what we are. What did those on the Titanic do when the ship was sinking? They all jumped off because they knew it just wasn't going to work anymore. And I don't mean church as an organic movement of fearlessly divine driven people who tenaciously chase after hope has failed, but the systems within which are killing the system. And I think it is a much needed death. If we can think of the church as a phoenix, then there is hope – there is always hope! Then maybe we need to come up with new terms and new words and new ideas for what we could be. I do have hope for that kind of future. And it lies in the future and not in the past. And I think a good place to start is with this incessant need for labels. Can we be honest? We need to get rid of them. They hurt. They purge. They destroy. They don't bring hope. Sometimes we spend so much of our energy trying to create ways to find who has the badge of salvation and who doesn't that we end up hurting people rather than helping them. How we choose what we say can have destructive consequences even when the intention of those words are meant to be healing. To determine the direction of someone else's soul primarily based on the utterance of a few words would reduce the person rehearsing them to nothing more than a puppet, and the person leading the prayer the puppeteer. The act of using words like salvation, hell, heaven, grace, forgiveness are ways in which we unknowingly support a diametric approach to God and religious discourse. These terms, though good, are inadequate in demonstrating the fierce love God has for all creation. If we spend all of our energies focusing on how to determine 'who's saved' and 'who's not saved', then the person dying of starvation, is still dying of starvation. Theological discourse doesn't stop AIDS from killing millions of people. We need something that practically meets the needs of the hurting people in the world that we encounter, not correct or incorrect rhetoric.

the universal for the ethnic.

The Pharisees were a religious sect within Judaism who had

24

chosen to follow all the Jewish laws to the letter. They wanted a small message for a small group of people. They mistook the universal for the ethnic. As I am sure we all have done. It means that we take a message that was intended for many and assume it is for the few. It seems that this happens quite a bit when we read scripture. The salvation of mankind being one example - some might think that when Jesus died he 'saved' only a predetermined amount of people. Others might think that all people have been redeemed and all are already accepted through the death and resurrection of Jesus. The danger is that we can also do the opposite, take what was meant for a certain group of people and make it applicable to everything in creation. One example, could be when we read the Ten Commandments, which are good and helpful. Although in context these were written as an initial convenant between God and the nation of Israel as a way to demonstrate their commitment to God. There is an inherent danger in decontextualizing our subjective interpretations of scripture and applying them to the lives of others, assuming that those we share our discoveries with need to follow our insights.

Jesus wanted to give God's message of hope to everyone, not just the Church. Organized claustrophobic religion was not his goal, if it was, he would have ended up with the Pharisees as his disciples.[11] But, those are not whom Jesus spent most of his time with. When we meet up with Jesus on his childhood hill and he begins to talk to the crowd about salt and light and being a city[12], he is addressing a mixed audience. There were men, women and children rallied together hoping for something different. His message would have sent ripples through the this Jewish society, who thought they were the chosen nation and that the message was all about being chosen and not about taking it out to the rest of the world[13].

cultural imagery.

Jesus employed distinct Jewish symbols because this was the context within which he lived. Take for example salt. Salt was used for many things in first-century Palestine. It was used to melt snow in the temple courts to allow others to come and make their necessary sacrifices. Salt was also a type of currency and very high in value. Essentially, Jesus is telling his audience that they, like currency [14], can effect systems within society for the better. That they too are high in value and that they are not their labels. A liberating message I think all of us might need to hear. This new society of Jesus didn't work on the assumptions of the existing systems in place. It looked at all people as vital contributors to the world. As important parts of creation. As a people who weren't valuable based on what they had or didn't have or whether they were sinful or sick. In the eyes of Jesus, all people were valuable. You and I are matter.

a group of nobodies.

I loved being team captain. it meant I could choose who I knew was in or out. I could choose people who I knew had what it took to get us the winning victory. And if we won, it meant we could all go and feed our faces at Pizza Hut to celebrate and then go join Weight Watchers to lose it all over again. (Ah, to be a part of the American dream! There wasn't a chance I was going to give that up.) I could slowly canvas the group of nobodies among the somebodies and try my best to separate the two and leave the leftovers for the apparent losing team. A follower of the Rabbi Jesus named Peter thought the same way.

He being a Jew, had this idea that the message of Jesus only extended to a few people. Peter mistook the universal for the ethnic and without knowing it, hijacked the message from within. Peter and Paul disputed over this very thing. Yet, he has a complete turn-around after that discussion, when Peter actually rethinks everything.

it means one time.

In his first letter to some Gentile Christians, Peter applies his newfound discoveries and says "For the Messiah also suffered for sins once for all, an innocent person for the guilty, so that he could bring you to God"[15]. Peter is explaining what he thinks is the universal significance of Christ's death on the cross for all of mankind. Peter is saying that Christ died once for all time. That word 'once' in the Hebrew is singular, it means one time. Peter was saying that there is never ever going to be a need for someone else God-like to have to come again and die in our place. It happened once and for all. When Jesus whispered the words on the cross, "it is finished!", this is in part what He was saying "It's all over now. We don't need to keep rehashing the gory details." Yet, if you walk into a church you will constantly hear words like repentance and forgiveness, which tend to be tripled with this almost mythical place of perpetual death and fire. I think the full message of forgiveness has been lost in the mail somewhere. The message of Christ's forgiveness has once again been hijacked from within.

Let's rewind a bit and meet Paul who was known by his title 'The Apostle', which means sent one. One of Paul's many roles was that he would advocate the murder of those who followed in the way of Jesus. He was convinced that what he was doing was a favor for God. He thought he was protecting the orthodox truth of his religion[16]. One day Paul was travelling to this city to go and kill some more 'heretics' and he had this ecstatic experience when Jesus turned the light bulb[17] on and Paul realized he messed it all up and literally changed his whole way of thinking. Sometimes it takes an event that drops you to your knees to help you realize that you might need to make some changes. If you ever hear Paul tell his story, he focuses on when He met Jesus. It was about him encountering Christ. And that looks different for each person.

sevartha (hope).

All of mankind have been made pure, holy and acceptable. This doesn't mean we don't get it wrong, it means that in each of us is the ability to get it right. And focusing on that is much more conducive to forward motion. And it allows us to go out and find creative ways to meet the needs of those in the world. To bring sevartha. if we focus on ourselves, others miss out on what God could give them through us. This is where the message should begin, not end. This is the message of sevartha. The gospel. The message of hope. The more we embrace this reality the more the world around us becomes more as it was intended to be. The gospel message says all people are free. Everyone. Right now. The story of Jesus doesn't end with our forgiveness, it starts there and invites us all to be a part of it. if this is all true then that would make everyone a new creation[18] as Paul once said so eloquently. What is Paul saying here and why does it matter in this context?

It's crucial to first understand that the Greek language is quite sophisticated and at times even leaves verbs out of its sentence structure. This means that sometimes we have to go through the whole of the letter before we can get the full message. After doing that, a better rendering might be: "if anyone is in Christ — New Creation!" Another point of view is that the verb is the subject. So it might sound like this: 'If anyone is in the messiah, the new creation has come!' Richard Liantonio 4 is an intercessory missionary and worship leader who explains it this way:

"... If this latter translation is correct – then 'being in the Messiah' is not simply an opportunity for a fresh start or a new chance to get things right (as great as that is). Being in Jesus means that one is a participant in the eschatological life of the restored and renewed heavens and earth even now. Some way and some how, through the Messiah, the God's future for the world, where peace, justice, life and joy reigns, has come forward and burst forth in the present time. This is not a "spiritualization" of eschatology. Rather, understanding the *radicality* of New Testament thought is grasping that the apostles believed this time of literal, cosmic, physical, eschatological fulfillment, the full restoration of heaven and earth, though yet remaining future, has nevertheless dawned in "the now." This restoration is already tasted by those who are 'in the Messiah.'"

The word Paul is using here, is *ktisis.* it means the sum of all things created. He is playing on the creation narrative, which is a typical Jewish way of writing. They had the principal of first reference, anytime you heard a word being used in someone's speech, it most likely alluded back to the first time it was being used. The first time the word creation popped up was in Genesis. He is telling his audience that they have been fully restored to what God had intended. That we are no longer living in the Genesis 3 reality, but we are in Genesis 1 from that point onwards. Now, that is *good news.* it doesn't mean we don't need God, it means that our relationship with Him is more interactive, interdependent and less co-dependent. it is also a reminder that we are all connected to the whole of creation. And that through the life of Jesus all of creation is in the process of renewal and we get to be a part of it all by making beneficial decisions about how much electricity we use or how much food we waste or how much we choose to buy into The more consumerism we embrace, the more blind we become. It makes us blind to the person next to us. Blind to poverty. Blind to the control we are under. Blind to the oppression we unintentionally agree with. Blind to the idea that more makes us more. Blind to the reality that from that point forward, our souls are slave to something that we can't see. The more corporate we become the less people matter. The more we emerge into a society of self-indulgence that 'looks out for number one', the more rapidly our worldview will become barbaric in how it chooses to respond to the needs of others. The more we take the less become, or as an unknown author once said, "He who buys what he does not need steals from himself." To be a new creation means we have to open our eyes to what's going on around us. That to truly love our neighbour means we have to be willing to go beyond ourselves to help those who might have become victims or perpetrators of this blindness. We have to stand in the gap. To be a new creation means we are living out this new identity in every way. But, you don't always hear that in a sermon.

hijacked.

There is an ancient story shrouded in poetic about one of the most famous Israeli battles in history and how their king meets up with a giant named Goliath in a Palestinian field for the future of their nation. At this time in history, their prophets would begin to speak of a messiah who was going to come through the lineage of David. This saviour was going to change everything. Some Rabbi's have translated this story to represent the warring reality between the Old Covenant and the New Convenant. Now the Old Covenant is summed up in the Ten Commandments given to Moses on Mt. Sinai. The New Covenant swallowed the Old Covenant in Christ's death. So, even before Jesus stepped into our world and invoked a new way to be human and a new 'covenant' (which alludes to a way of living), there was already talk about how things could be better. How things as they are aren't good enough. How maybe the old is hiding the new from us. Maybe it is our responsibility to make sure that the world as it is and the world as it should be, meet. And the same goes for the Church as it is and as it could be. Our potential is waiting and our theological views could be the enemy that is keeping us from the very transformation we desire and are seeking. The question is are we willing to wade through our own worldviews and dive into others to find what we're looking for?

the trail.

I love to hike. If there is some inviting vista hidden with a plethora of trees, I will race to get there. It becomes my only focus, where all my energies lie – getting to whereI need to be. And as Iget nearer to the goal, I find I sometimes lose out on what's around me. Once I hit the beautiful panoramic view, it reminds me that that things are much bigger than they appear on the trail. If we all can agree that we are in discovery of truth, then truth would be this trail. We might call the trail "Christian" truth, Buddhist truth and the list goes on. But the panoramic view we could call Truth, itself.

Sometimes our own discoveries of truth can even limit us from finding Truth. Thomas who was one of Jesus' friends experienced this as well. Most of the time, he gets a bad rap as a guy who doubted Jesus. But questions are good.

We need to recapture the art of the question. I doubt quite a bit. Doubting is essential to our faith because it makes all the things that are hard to believe, believable. I think Thomas wanted more of Jesus, and he didn't care who knew about it. He didn't just want to hear about the Messiah coming back to life, he wanted to talk to him, eat with him, share life with his friend who had been gone for way too long.Who wouldn't? Before Thomas received his unfair nickname (*The Doubter*), he had a conversation with Jesus that demonstrated that he too was a trail-walker.

changing our message.

Jesus is hanging out with some friends and He tells them He is getting ready to go back home. And Thomas wants to get Jesus' address and phone number to come and visit. Thomas was seeking the "4 Steps to Peace With God" [19] or the "12 Steps to Recovery". Not that those things are wrong in and of themselves, but the problem is that we tend to be creatures of habit who can't live without our habits and Jesus knew this. Jesus responds to

Thomas's question by saying that He is "…the way, the truth and the life…". This is where truth has been mangled and decontextualized. We have to recapture the Aramaic message of Jesus to understand what His message was and how it changes our message, if anything, and what we do with it.

The Hebrew word for way is 'derek'. It means someone who is of moral character. It also means to journey. Essentially, he says: "I am the journey". But even more so, he is telling Thomas that he has showed him how to live. How to breath in this new way. That life isn't about some systemic approach that we tear to pieces. He goes on to say that He is the truth. The Hebrew word for truth means concrete. Something solid. Something to hold onto that doesn't move. Something you can count on. Jesus is challenging Thomas to let go of his innate desire to have all the answers and trust him. To let go and to get to know Jesus on His terms. This is a different message to the one we have been given. He is also demonstrating to Thomas who and what he could be. That he too could embody truth. Maybe even something deeper than that, is that we all can embody truth. That truth isn't about one person or one religion, but that it is a journey to our self-discovery in God. Or even a collective self-discovery of what we can become. When we spend all of our time trying to dissect what Jesus might have meant, we lose sight of what he was saying to all of us. This also doesn't change the importance of Jesus and how we learn from him; it does change how we've been taught to see him though.

Jesus was inviting Thomas into a new kind of relationship, one that didn't depend on sacrifice or duty. But a relationship encompassed by love.

A divine romance that involved two lovers. God and man, constantly chasing after one another in relationship. We as people find comfort in systems and habits and our own pet ways of doing things. Sometimes we get so protective of them, we don't let anyone know about them. Sometimes we get angry if someone comes in and messes up our rhythm.

Jesus knew this too.

Another take on what Jesus said in John 14 verse 6 would be something like this: "I am not found in your habits, i am not found in your rhetoric, I am not found in your systematic theologies or theology for that matter"[20] Jesus invites us all into relationship and for those who think they've figured Him out, He invites them back into the simplicity of the candlelight dinner and dance.

Jesus is this sort of map we get to travel through.

A map shows some details of the journey in mind. If you look at a country or state map it might give certain distances between each destination or place. If you look closer it might give you highways or interstates. Some maps might even give you restaurants or places of entertainment depending on the genre and style of the map. The map can only give you so much though. A map doesn't show you the people, car, houses, or the televisions in the house. It doesn't make the map any less of a map, because it is the map being the map; giving you details of the destination or goal.

Jesus points us back to God. In several places he uses the phrase "Kingdom of God", rather than the kingdom of Jesus. In one verse he also says something like this, "I am here to do the will of Him who sent me [21]" and so on. Jesus came here to show us God in skin. To show us how to be God in our skin. How to embrace the divine within. To introduce a new way to be human. To show us how to connect with God. To be the ultimate example of God on earth for all of mankind.

The map shows us how to get to the destination. In this context, God is the destination. If we spend all our time worshipping the map, and spending all of our time dissecting the map, then we might never get to the destination. Especially when the "map" is telling us to look towards the destination.

When Jesus said that He was the truth He was inviting people into a curious kind of relationship of ongoing discovery. The ancient Jews believed that truth was unfolding rather than something to be violently conquered or colonialized. It's this perpetual rollercoaster that might begin with scripture, but is not contained only in a compilation of ancient pages. It invites us into the awareness that the ride doesn't stop there. It involves a lot of wrestling and journeying through mountains and valleys. It's a red carpet being rolled out, yet, the red carpet doesn't have an end … it continues on and on.

truth is something we can join.
We have a blood-thirsty history of proclaiming truth in the name of God when it was realistically more about personal ethics than truth. Truth isn't a right or wrong. Truth isn't defined by morality. Sure, there are traces of truth but is so much more significant than one thing or one religion for that matter. Truth isn't an absolute philosophical concept. Maybe it starts there, but it is more of an ongoing discovery and rediscovery of the person of Jesus. This too looks different for each person. Jesus' call was for all people to come and join him. It is up to them whether they want to follow or not.

A friend recently reminded me that Jesus wasn't about getting everyone to necessarily be a disciple or follower. Jesus was more about getting his message of hope, love, peace, grace and restoration out to everyone. His goal wasn't to sell an agenda, but to live out what he believed in. How do you do that? By passing it along. He doesn't invite the woman caught in adultery to join the crew, or the woman near Jacob's well to jump on the bandwagon. He doesn't tell the rich young ruler that he is lost; no, he lets him walk away. Jesus' desire is for those that follow to share their discoveries with everyone they meet. How? Transference. Human touch. Action. Compassion is the new transformation. It is the art of being Christ everywhere we go. Truth isn't about forcing people to join. Truth doesn't need converts. Truth desires a friendship that starts by letting go of all of our preconceived notions and ideas that seem to stand in the way. Truth is bigger than any idea. So, what's happened to it then?

Maybe the message of Truth has also been hijacked from within.

When we begin to see things as bigger than our own thoughts and assumptions, it creates a lot more room for God to be God on His terms. It allows us to see things that are impossible as possible. It also absolves us from chains that bind us to a static way of thinking.

As I am sitting staring out the window basking in my attraction habitual dualism, I am envisioning truth as a person, and if it is a person, this might be a letter I would write to it:

"Dear Truth,

I know we've often missed each other. Sometimes we pass each other in the hallway at home. Or down the street while crossing paths with the guy who holds the cardboard sign. I know so many throughout history have fought for you in the name of their deity. Some believe you are their deity. Some would kill for you. Some already have. So, what's the big deal? Why are you such a hot topic all the time? What makes you the point of all the stories of all histories of all people in the world? Can you enlighten me what you are? How to find you, and why you seem so hard to grasp?

I thought we were friends. And at times we have walked hand in hand through the green foliage of the nearby forests. We have danced and sipped on wine together over a candelight dinner. We have shared so many wonderful moments that, even if I tried, I couldn't forget. I wouldn't want to. It just seems you don't know how you feel about me or where you stand on who I am. Is that true? I feel like you are more committed to betraying me and my sensibilities and my innate sense of right and wrong. Maybe we've crowded you on your search to find who you are meant to be. For this, I am truly sorry. But, it does seems like you have come to the conclusion that it is better for you to just be yourself. And I have to be honest, that is a bit selfish and unfair. Because like so many before me, I think I should have a right to define you, to mold you into a creation of my own design.

I think I might find you in my favorite television show, and sometimes like a guest appearance you surprise me by showing up there. Or in a song. Or in the wind. Or in a conversation I don't want to leave or maybe one I wish I was never part of. I like it when I find you in the setting sun while I am sitting on the roof waiting for the mythical green band to peek-a-boo its way back down into the horizon. That word myth has got me thinking…Have we made you up? Or did you make us up? Are you for real? Are we all just wasting our time. Is it true, what they say that you are only found in a journey? Not just in one book. Not just in one sacred verse. Not in one place. But that you decide to hide yourself in many places. That we have to go and find you. Are we getting it wrong? So many are afraid of that question. They want to be sure of you, but just don't know how. So, most (as I have been known to) choose the illusion of controlling you and who and what you should be. If I can lend one piece of advice on your journey Truth - don't let them."

mission.

Jesus invites us all to be intentional people. People with a purpose.

Why do we meet with people?

Not to get them to some institution with a cross as its logo. We meet them because all of us are made to be in relationship. We meet people because we want to know them and they want to know us. To know and to be known is a defenselessly divine act because it can move us into a kind of unguarded territory we have never experienced before. Where we get to embrace the uknown aspects of this new event we are a part of. However, we don't meet them because we want to somehow sell them Jesus. We don't meet them because we are guilted into a pew quota, or trying to get more and more numbers into the corporation of Christianity[22]. This is what mission has become.

Maybe we can come to a better understanding of what might have been misunderstood for the last 2,000 years. Mission isn't some idea where we try and gain new ground. Mission isn't a way to try and convince people about something that is lacking in their lives, it is to introduce them into a new way of life and there is a difference. Everyday we have various types of media fighting to get our attention to inform us that we need more to feel like we're more. Wouldn't it be a sad moment if we found out we were advocating marketing models and applying them to something that was intended to be a fluid movement? Maybe we need a new approach all together. Maybe the missions we do weren't intended to be what they are. Maybe we need to give up our intentions all together. Maybe a better alternative might be unethical heterology. Unethical heterology is this idea that says we should be able to come into conversations without the intention of changing the morals of another. Where we leave behind agendas and spend all of our energy searching for the image of God within that person. If there are any, it is to solely to connect to that person. not to convert them. but to learn from them. to be transformed. and sure, if they get something out of it, great, but it isn't our intention to 'school' them. Mission could be re-introduced as something we live out in relationship with God and the rest of creation. Where we interact with atheists, Muslims, Christians and others to find ways to practically heal the world. Mission is something we are part of rather than something we do. Mission is about being the movement wherever we are, it isn't about how many people we are meeting on a daily basis or how we are directing our conversation towards conversion. When we approach the concept of missions with this approach in mind, people stop becoming human and are reduced to nothing more than real estate that we fight over to close the deal. Maybe we can reframe our thinking on Mission and move into a movement where we adopt defiant hope as our tagline and desire to be a people who seek contexts where we can inclusively implement shalom, love, grace, and resurrection as we live out what we believe. Maybe mutual reciprocity is a better word, because it assumes we can learn from those we engage with just as much as we can teach. It also allows space to accept that the idea of truth is the tension between the two people discussing their worldviews. Mutual reciprocity focuses all of its energy on the person rather than theological enterprise which tends to reduce conversation down to some numerical value.

redefine.
Rome was a politically oppressive country that proclaimed their peace through victory. They wanted to make sure that their worldview was the only one that stood up and they would kill anyone who saw differently. This was their 'evangelism'. Then Jesus stepped in and began speaking of a different kind of evangelism. It was a new way to see things, a call to a new and different way of life. it was a reality to live in and be a part of, (not a prayer for salvation). We have taken Christ's political message and domesticated it with church language. We have also adopted the Roman techniques to make sure everyone around us knows that we are right and they are wrong. And when we do this, people get hurt.

Although this may not be the intention, some people believe 'mission' is solely about colonializing whoever it comes into contact with. I think we need to revise our narrative worldviews. We need to understand that Christianity is part of a meta-narrative that has been going on before its own discovery. A meta-narrative is a story *about* a story [23], it is the larger context within which all history is being told. A simple example would be that a student goes to school to learn so they could get a job. The meta-narrative for the student would be getting the job after going to school, to get money to help care for his family, the school which leads to the job and then leads to the family, these are all aspects of meta-narrative. The danger in legitimizing meta-narratives as a way to interpret history is that it advocates only one version of true history rather than allowing space for other sides to share their experiences. That is why the Bible, as a historical document, is quite peculiar because it is told by those who are *part* of a meta-narrative, not the ones leading its development. When I use the term meta-narrative, I don't mean to suggest the meta-narratives of the past which were directly connected with the bigger and stronger oppressing the smaller and weaker. I think that is part of the narrative that needs to be scrapped. I would suggest that this new approach to narratives and rewriting them includes rewriting the terminology[24] we have been using. It seems that the language that was used in the days of Jesus induced a spirit of inclusivity, but now it has been used to spur on a spirit of exclusivity. One reason being that the language has become a bit outdated and archaic in light of the generational gaps that are easily apparent by walking down the street. I would say that this new narrative has to be relevant to the world within which it lives. I would also add that another reason why we need to change how we see the world, Christianity, evangelism and many other things within the faith, is simply because it just doesn't work anymore. Think about this in terms of buying a car. If a car's tires are becoming bald, we can buy new ones and it would be fine. But if a car's engine begins to fail, which tends to most likely lead to smaller problems along with it (e.g., the fuse box breaks, a light goes out, the heating is on the fritz etc.) then the better thing to do is buy a new car, not rebuild the old one. This is what Martin Luther King Jr was attempting to do; he was stating that we need a new car. Let me explain a bit more. We need a new perspective on what we believe and why we believe it. Some of this new perspective might need some spring cleaning. We might need to leave some things at the wayside and pick some others up and maybe even reintegrate some ancient ones. I think this is also what might need to happen with Mission. I think we need a new car. When Jesus told the disciples to go and 'teach' all nations. At the root verb of teach (whether in Hebrew or Greek) is also the same word 'to learn'. So maybe being evangelists is also about being evangelised. Not just merely teaching people but also learning from them as well. Peter Rollins is the founder of the experimental collective gathering in Ireland called Ikon.[25] One of their many experiments is that they invite people from different faith traditions to join their gatherings and participate in evangelizing (interactively sharing their views) the members who are being evangelized as well (listening and learning). I think this is an important part of understanding what it means to go into all the world as the author of the book of Matthew records Jesus saying. In the Greek, the word for 'teach' carries the same meaning as learn. In this new light evangelism then becomes something we participate in on a daily basis, anytime we learn something we are being evangelized, anytime we are teaching it is evangelizing. I was invited to speak at an Easter service about 20 minutes down the road and in the middle of the talk with the congregation someone informed me about soil science, something I had never heard of before. It's not a subject I would personally Google even if I had free time, but that day I learned something new, I was evangelized. Maybe evangelism isn't about simply telling others what we think they might need to hear, but its also listening to their stories as well. Then it becomes about how we are being changed rather than the unnecessary pressure of who and how many we are changing.

good news.

Sometimes the good news in Christianity sounds something like this: "You are a sinner and you're going to hell, but Jesus died for you so you don't have to go to hell, so ask him to come into your life and save you and then thank him and say 'Amen." I don't mean to sound irreverent, this was the good news that was shared with me, but I do think its incredibly lacking and condescending. So, what was the good news then?

People like Emperor Augustus would have used the phrase "good news" as another phrase to signify their political agenda. When Christ steps on the scene, He begins talking about a new kind of good news that is about an almost mythical kind of Kingdom that is transferred from one person to another through love rather than an oppressive urgency. If you look at how Christ interacted with people, you might be able to see that we have lost our way. He peers into their being and sees the best they could be and releases that in any way possible.

the back of the book.

I have never been a big fan of math. I was the guy waiting for the teacher to turn her back so I could slowly peer over my neighbor's shoulder to find the answer I needed, so I didn't have to repeat the course. Thanks to all those people! As I got older, math got that much more complicated and so did the answers. But, what was even more exciting was the discovery that the answers were in the back of the book. (Okay, so there were only the odd numbers, but it was enough for me to feel okay about the numerical journey ahead.) Plus, I could depend on my unsuspecting tutors to help me get through the next year of math. I felt okay after knowing there was a good chance i might pass my class. Knowledge is a very powerful thing. It whispers to our need for safety. Labels make sense of things. Some things that would probably be better off left unlabeled! Calling someone a sinner gives us a subconscious sense of superiority. Labeling people puts us on the pedestal. If you stand up on the chair of psychology, then someone who has family issues and has a hard time connecting with people in general, is labeled as "anti-social". For those in medicine, if there is a person who has trouble controlling their shaking hand, it might be assumed that they have an early onset diagnosis of Parkinsons. For those that are religious, we might look at someone who believes something that is outside of our sphere of theology and label them a pagan or a heretic. Now, let me say that labels in and of themselves aren't bad; it's the malice with which they are used that is the problem. It is the intention behind the words that really give the end phrase the ultimate value. Could it be possible that God has labeled everyone as being fully restored as well as being restored?

house party.

The Jews knew how to party. At times, they could have easily rivaled some high school parties today.

Seven days.
Alcohol.
Music.
Dancing.
Poetry.
Art.

One of the parties (they used the word festival) was entitled the Feast of the Tabernacles. Practicing Jews know this now as Sukkot. The word means dwelling or abode. it was a dwelling festival or a "house party". They would grab some wood, nails, and a hammer to create this temporary living space. It was a reminder that God was always going to be there for them. A reminder for them that He was their shelter when they were rescued from Egypt.They were instructed to create a dwelling with no walls as a reminder that they should maintain a spirit of constant hospitality... even to foreigners and outsiders.

Even in the early days of of mankind, God's heart for the marginalized was made clear in the architecture of Jewish festivals. These Jews carried a responsibility to make sure to invite those passing through. A place to stay. A place to call home. Hospitality. They would also make a roof with an opening in the middle to give them a skylight to the heavens above, to remind them that God wasn't very far away. They would have this party and invite fellow house party members to come over and enjoy themselves and sit around campfires and share stories of how God rescued them and how they barely made it out alive. There were humans connecting with one another from completely different backgrounds. And God was for that. He was there. "...when two or more are gathered...I am there"[26] They would drink and salute God because He chose them to be his message-bearers. There has been a recent resurgence of interest in the end times (the apocalypse) and how it all is going to play out in the end. What's even more interesting is that each Jewish festival didn't just signify a remembering or looking back, but also a looking forward.

everybody goes.

Jewish Rabbinical Scholars say that each party or festival represents an event in the end time scheme. The House Party falls into the point in our future history where God brings people to His Kingdom. Some scholars debate that it could mean that all people get to be a part of the New Jerusalem. That instead of only some receiving invitations to the party, everyone gets to come. We say things like "when we get to heaven" or "when I go to heaven". Maybe the end times were never about "one day when", but a series of letters from an author in a particular time and space that we infused with this deep hope that God is going to come through. Maybe it was a metaphor for how we are the ones who represent God in the diverse acts of coming through. If we focus so much on then, we will never be here. This point of view on the festivals is very indicative of how the Jews saw the world. Everything had a hidden meaning. Eating wasn't just eating. Walking wasn't just walking. The rain wasn't just the rain. It was a reminder that heaven and earth were connected. The wind wasn't just the wind, it was a reminder of a God who moves, who breathes and is alive. Everything we do has meaning, everything we say and even how we say it has meaning. Meaning is every where; we just have to look for it. But the danger is when we take things and try to make them into something that they are not.

piracy.

We live in a world of knock-off's. Piracy is one of the largest criminal activities out there. It is the process of taking something that is authentic and making copies of it and then repackaging it as if it is the real deal.

It happens in the art world. It would be like taking the Mona Lisa and making an exact replica but selling it off as the real thing. The world of celluloid has found a way into the Church.

In the world of computer piracy, people have found ways to copy movies from the big screen to DVDs. Numerous articles have been recently on how people are fined vast amounts for making and selling DVD's as if the actors walked right off the screen. Claiming what they have is the real thing when it's not.

Sometimes this even happens in our pulpits. We've pirated the message of Jesus and made it into something it's not. We have turned Jesus into someone who is more concerned about views and less concerned about pain. We have transformed God into nothing less than Santa Claus who advocates war and nationalism. Maybe we need to be honest about what our convictions have become. Maybe we need to betray some of the things we have come to call 'faith' to find out what Jesus meant when he shared his heart with the crowd. This is the hardest part, coming to terms with the reality that we have had a hand in creating something completely oppressive.

We need a drastic realignment of how we approach God. We need new questions and a new journey that takes us into places unknown. Into the corners where we have come to fear the most. A movement where people are willing to question everything - to scandalously dream out- loud about all the possibilities of what could be if everyone joined in on the conversation. In this new reformation, there could be an ethos of dynamic inclusion whereby all people, from all backgrounds and ages, get to help dream up the kind of world that God had intended. Maybe it could be a movement of people dedicated to seeing that poverty is evil, not right or wrong theology. Maybe this new realignment could usher in an era of progressive change. In evolutionary sociology there is this theory that presumes that social learning can only benefit us when the landscape transforms around us. Maybe, love could be the new landscape and the driving force behind all we do. Maybe, just maybe.

Fairies and Frogs

"Every generation needs a new revolution."
– Thomas Jefferson

In the movie *V for Vendetta,* Evey was this mild-mannered girl who lived her every day life in down-town London. She was a good citizen. Until she met a mysterious character by the name of 'V'. This ominous figure named V believed the government had become too powerful for its own good. He wanted things to change and he was willing to go to any lengths necessary to make sure that that kind of change was going to happen. Even if that meant the destruction of systems and structures that were the ultimate icons of oppressive power. He invited Evey (through a series of tests) and others to join a new kind of conspiracy that changed the face of England and history itself.

V was starting a revolution. One that almost anyone could be a part of, if they wanted to. One that would flip the world as we know it on its head.

Jesus was trying to do the same. Or was He?

Revolution can be defined as "a fundamental shift in power" It tends to be directly related to governments and their infra-structures. We have many of these in our history books. The American Revolution being one of them. But, did Jesus come to violently descend from heaven to overthrow the Roman government · Some ? No. But, some of the Jews, including his followers thought he did so. But, on a political level, Jesus did not come to be a revolutionary. If we choose to use the word broadly, in the sense of a movement started by a person or a group of people with the hope of affecting change in a society for the benefit of the population, then Jesus definitely came to bring that kind of revolution to all of humanity. Most historical revolu-tions have occurred at the hand of those who have been the winners in history. They have been the authors of the meta-narrative. The sky is always blue.

In one place the revolution of Jesus is anti-revolutionary to all the oppressive meta-narratives that have graced our history books. It is even counter-cultural to its own ideology.

the sky is always blue.

Jesus says that He came to bring a sword not peace. For the Jews, the sword was linked with Rome and their way of advancing themselves. It would have created feelings of uneasiness and restlessness. It was a semiotic symbol used by Jesus to represent social unrest. And the peace in that verse pertains to social order. So, Jesus came to upset the system. To challenge the every day expectations and status quo of the Jewish people and the Roman world. So, this movement of Jesus was intended to turn the world upside down. If you've ever hung upside down for any period of time you know all kinds of things go wrong. Blood rushes to your head. You might lose your lunch. You might even pass out. But to be sure, your sense of reality is disrupted. So by this definition, can we at least agree that Jesus came to start a social revolution and reinterpret reality in order to introduce a new kind of reality?

Jesus culture.

The social revolution of Jesus is more explicit than Marxism, although there are hints of Karl Marx all over the movement of Jesus. According to the Professor of Anthropology at California State University in Long Beach, "Marx and Jesus agree that humanity is approaching a fundamental transformation[27]." It is imperative to hear that this is not advocating that Jesus was a communist in the pervasive sense of the word, but that there are similarities within the movement and philosophies of Jesus and Karl Marx that saw a change that needed to happen in the form of a revolution. I think Jesus could have agreed with Marx's assessment of religion as an opiate for the masses. A quick fix for problems too big for a quick fix. There are some brilliant people who are doing some great things in response to the reality that religion as an idea is waning. They are creating a necessary revolution. One built on love, hope and redemption. Jesus invites us into this kind of revolution. One that changes everything. And even at times creates more unrest than peace in the conventional sense. Jesus would have wine with AIDS victims, some of his friends would have been part of the homosexual community, and others might have included drug users. And they weren't sinners, they were people who had value. There was room for everyone at his living room table. Maybe that's why he was a carpenter; he wanted to create chairs for dialogue[28]. Scripture was written by those within this culture, and by a few of those outside of it, who caught on to the heart of Jesus' message. Some people read scripture and pick and pull out their favourite verses creating a theological niche that works with their own worldview. The buffet approach to scripture. Others might think of the pages of the Bible as more of a car manual where they go to get instructions on how to live and how not live and how to see the world. Although seeing scripture from this worldview has its benefits, it is incredibly anaemic. It tends to focus on only one aspect of scripture. I think it is good to recognize that the Bible was written by people who interacted with the divine and then wrote down their experiences. Their intention may not have been for us to canonize every move or word of God that drips from their lips. it is a book of discovery on how others saw God and how they came to their conclusions. But even more so, it was a collection of pages by authors who always thought God was bigger than the Bible. It is crucial to remember that our own worldview may also be affected by what happened to us as a child. What happened to us in school? What is happening to us even now? Who we are affects how we read what we read. Whether it's scripture or People's magazine. Some Christians might read a verse like John 3:16 which says, "For God so loved the world that he gave his one and only Son, that whoever believes in him shall not perish but have eternal life" as a manifesto that excludes people. But the Aramaic and Greek word for 'world' means all things on earth and in the universe. Not just people. When Jesus spoke of the universe it didn't mean only a select few people, but every single living and created thing on earth is to be restored. it also depends on how you define what Jesus meant by 'believe' or 'belief systems'. Some people approach scripture with the "sky is always blue" belief system. Where no matter how many times one might say the sky is purple, pink or green – to them the sky is always blue because science and reason have proven it so. Others might choose to approach scripture from a more creative angle, a worldview where not everything is mapped out just yet. An unfinished blueprint. A blueprint we all get to help finish by living out scripture now. And how we react to poverty, injustice, anger, abuse, hatred and greed will determine what the end of the book will look like one day. This isn't to say that there isn't any value in the "the sky is always blue approach", it just means we need to find ways to look beyond our own approaches and create new ways to restore the world as it was meant to be. Beliefs become useless if they don't lead to a common movement that everyone can be a part of. This overeager search for the unknown aspects of truth creates a fear of the unknown. Some psychologists define the fear of the unknown as a psychosis. A psychiatric split in the mind where the world will only feel safe again, once we know the answers. It's much like the process of paranoia. Where people become fearful of all the possibilities of things that haven't happened yet. Our search and attempts at colonizing truth may find some of its origins in the period known as the Enlightenment. A time where systems, thoughts and structures were being questioned and redefined in the hope of helping society as a whole. This aspect of the Enlightenment in the here in and now has resurfaced in some circles within Christianity and other religions. Some people know this philosophy as post-modernism, which can't really be explained in a few words. One of the features of post-modernism is that it allows room to ask questions and also provides a lot of space to find out possibilities for answers. It sometimes even allows the opportunity to realize that maybe answers might just minimize the beautiful scandalous attributes that the search brings. We must be willing to let go of our knowledge to discover who God is on his terms. When we find Him there, we must be willing to let go of all of the things our human minds have tried to rationalize about Him. It's is scary thing to have to let go of the very things you've called truth for so long. But do we quiver if someone asks 'is the sky blue?' no, because the majority says it is blue. What about when Copernicus challenged the makeup of the universe? A lot of people were up in arms on this one. Why? Because it challenged the fabric of their belief system. It challenged their reality as they knew and accepted it. New ideas force a sort of transitory change or at least the option to accept it. I am sure Copernicus didn't mean to put himself in a position where he might die for what he found out. He was just sharing what he found. from the 'transcript' of what he shares, it doesn't seem that he came in 'all guns blazing', but that he did want eagerly share his discovery out of more than anything — excitement. Why is it we're okay with the discoveries of Copernicus but don't allow much room for anything else? When it comes to new discoveries about the person of Jesus or the bible, we get nervous, angry, frustrated and in a defensive posture. I don't think its' because of our allegiance to Jesus. If there was ever a person in our faith-tradition who was against stereotypical dogmatic practices and doctrinal beliefs about god, it was Jesus. We simply fear change even though we know we need it. This kind of fear causes destructive movements like the Crusades to happen. This kind of fear impedes any movement at all.

story.

People like a good story. The tendency is to hear the word story and think of folklore or a simple bedtime fairytale, but this is so much deeper than fairies and frogs. Rabbi Nachman of Bratzlev, a Jewish Mystic said this about God and story: "God made man because he loves stories." One of the most popular leisure activities for families and friends to do is to go to the movies. To get lost in two hours of story. Author Barry Lopez[29] says this about story "If stories come to you, care for them. And learn to give them away where they are needed. Sometimes a person needs a story more than food to stay alive." Stories aren't luxuries we get to hear at bedtime, its part of it sure, but story is a deeper reality than just that. Story is something that is the reality we are all a part of and the reality we get to carry on. It is our legacy. Without story we are all fictional characters being told what to do. I think we have forgotten that we get to help write the story. I imagine God sitting up in his comfy black leather couch sipping on his Caramel Frappucino enthralled by whom He has created and how we are all learning what it means to walk in the light of knowing that He has made us. And we are all learning this. We are fumbling toward ecstasy. Like author Donald Miller once said in a sermon, "God wants to write a good story with us...[30]" I think we have lost the art of telling a good story. I think we need to recapture this art or we will all slip into the art of just surviving. For most, life is about getting by. I am sure there is a place in the story for moments like that, but, I don't think we were meant to merely survive. We were meant for so much more. And this realization inspires us to write stories of hope. Of peace. Of grace. Of resurrection. Madeleine L'Engle once said this about story: "It's no coincidence that just at this point in our insight into our mysteriousness as human beings struggling towards compassion, we are also moving into an awakened interest in the language of myth and fairy tale. The language of logical arguments, of proofs, is the language of the limited self we know and can manipulate. But the language of parable and poetry, of storytelling, moves from the imprisoned language of the provable into the freed language of what I must, for lack of another word, continue to call "faith." There is something deep within us all that is aware, awakened and moved into the reality that there is more to life than what we now live. We have this longing question that keeps us awake at night, "Why am I alive? What am I here for?" These are the sheep we count as we nod off to find answers in the dreams we have yet to dream. That the world is not as it should be. That there is more. And that knowledge, keeps us searching for what that more looks like. All the while, as we continue on our search, there are a soundtrack of lyrics on repeat, playing in the disco of our head beckoning us on with the words like "...I still haven't found what I'm looking for..." This is the art of the story that we get drawn into when Jesus arrives on the scene and begins sharing stories of how life is more than what there currently is. And I think we can all agree that we all have those days where it feels like there could be more.

touching the surface.
Jesus told this story that would have been heard many times before, but He decided to change the characters to make His point. In fact, we have probably heard this many times before. Sometimes it's too easy to pass over something we have become comfortable with. It is the story of the Good Samaritan. We tend to tell this story to reinforce the idea of compassion being the central marker of someone who follows Jesus. And this thought is good but barely touches the surface at what is really going on here. Let's take into consideration why Jesus even told the story. There was a teacher of the law, this guy would have known the in's and out's of the Jewish law. He asked 'what must I do to inherit eternal life?' So, this is the leading question that compels Jesus to tell this remake of what would have been known

culturally as the good Jew. This is a dominant aspect of the story that tends to get glossed over. But, I think if we dig a bit deeper here, we might find a lot more going on than just a message about compassion. Now, eternal life, heaven and Kingdom of God tend to be used interchangeably here, meaning 'life of the ages' or life as it was meant to be. So, essentially this teacher is asking how He can join in on the movement of Jesus. Being a teacher of the law, he would have known the Torah which has an immensely high view of human life. Even after the supposed fall of humanity. Jesus is making a commentary on Leviticus 19:18 where the Jewish people are told to love their neighbours. Which is another question that is brought up by this teacher. "Who is my neighbour?" And Jesus redraws the boundaries to even include the Samaritan as their neighbour. In the Jewish culture, a Samaritan was a racial enemy. Someone who didn't fit in and was disliked. We can all probably think of someone we just can't get along with, in this case that is the protagonist in the Samaritan story. He's the good guy. Now, when the Jew heard this story, the third person wasn't supposed to be an outsider, it was supposed to be a Jew.

This story had been circulating around long before Jesus stepped on the scene. But Jesus changed the story. Sometimes we need a change in our story to fully understand it. Jesus then chooses to use the Samaritan, who was a racial outcast as well as a cultural enemy of the Jew. Samaritans who used to be Jews themselves until the two kingdoms split in the Old Testament. Jesus actually never gets around to answering the question. He challenges the inquisitor to be a neighbour to everyone. Further along in the story, we are told that the Samaritan takes the injured man to an inn and pays two denarii and any other costs incurred. He overextended himself for the sake of a stranger. For an outsider. The place where the injured guy stayed is loosely translated from the Greek into what we know as an inn or hotel. Since Jesus spoke Aramaic, he most likely used the word *funduq* instead

, which roughly translates into a *hostel*. If you walk into a hotel and then walk back out onto the street and walk into a hostel, you will see that there are visible differences, even in what is provided. This difference would have been recognizable to a Jew. So, why the big deal on the separation of words? Because a funduq was a place where all people from all walks of life would come and share life together, sometimes even share beds. It was a place of common ground. Very different to our churches today. This is what Jesus was essentially commenting on. It was the exclusive state of the synagogue that Jesus was directly dealing with here. He was challenging them to extend their compassion into their practices and every belief. Maybe we could learn from them today. In fact, in some of the early writings about the funduq there were stories of warring tribes and family members who would end up meeting in these mysterious places of peace and walk away in complete reconciliation. People from different faith traditions would enter through opposite entrances and end up walking out of the same one. Isn't that what we should be doing? Reconciling people. Healing broken relationships. Bringing peace where there seems to be none. This is the potential Jesus saw and was trying to draw out through this story. Jesus also uses currency in the story that seems to be nothing more than just money used in a transaction, but if you dive deeper into the narrative there is much more here.

the outsider saves.

Two denarii was the amount the Samaritan paid for the Jew. Two denarii was a direct reference to the half-shekel atonement. At the age of 13, a young Jewish child went from being a boy to a man and one of the many responsibilities of a man in that culture was to pay a temple tax. The temple tax was specifically reserved to purchase animals for the typical once-a-year sacrifice that the priest would enact for everyone on their behalf. His action would atone for the sins of others. Jesus is playing on the issue of atonement. Of being absolved from our sins. Here in the story though, it isn't the priest who absolves the victim, it is the Samaritan. The outsider. The one that society or the holy ones have chosen to label and mistreat.The homosexual. He atones for the victims' sin. it's as if Jesus is saying, larger than right or wrong, than sin or no sin, the one thing that can absolve the sins of another is hidden in the act of compassion. And anyone can join in on this movement of compassion. There is hope that we all can be a people dedicated to not merely seeing the need of someone else and walking by, but that we all, as the human race can fight indifference with compassion and grace. This is just one of many multi-faceted invitations in the story of the Samaritan who saves.

unclean ones.

Jesus is having a conversation with some of the outsiders and some of the religious leaders started gossiping under their breath about how it seems like Jesus is hanging out with all the wrong people. Jesus overhears some of their snarly commentary and starts to tell a story about 100 sheep. Numbers are never just numbers in Jewish writing. They were poets. They intended their words to be dripping with alternative meanings. The number 100 pertains to the selection process of God's chosen people. It was a direct reference at their thought that they were special because God chose them. It was a number of perfection and wholeness. But something went wrong in the story. And the audience would have anticipated some sort of occurrence, but maybe not the one that was coming. He was telling a story using their language, not trying to create a theology. I think it is important to take in the reality that Jesus didn't sit and wonder if one day people might create some systematic holy writ along with a system of beliefs out of what He said. He was just being Jesus. It's almost as if we walk around with a camera scrutinizing every move of Jesus and not letting him breathe. We have become the Jesus paparazzi with the intent of spreading Jesus all over the theological tabloids. If that is the case, then Jesus is here for nothing more than our pseudo-interests and our desire to be entertained.

borrowing your friends chariot.

As I shared earlier, the idea of repentance in scripture tends to be aimed at the followers of God. In first-century Palestine it was rude to blame someone for something. If you borrowed your friend's chariot and lost it. You wouldn't say you lost the chariot. Your friend wouldn't say *you* lost the chariot. You both would say that the chariot *got* lost. The implications are hilarious. And so Jesus starts the story out by saying "Suppose one of you...", so within a few words of the story, He is already incriminating them for their way of thinking by interjecting a cultural taboo into the story. In the book of Ezekiel, God romantically nicknames Israel as His sheep and He their shepherd. He promises to care for them and watch out for them like shepherds do. Jesus becomes the shepherd in this story and this shepherd goes for those outside the fold. Essentially, Jesus redraws the the boundaries again. He basically tells them that now the new sheep are the ones He chases after. This would have been another insult. Jesus isn't attempting an assault on all of their sensibilities (although, at times this does seem the case), in the sharing of his new vision for the world; there will be things that will naturally have to change and this is what Jesus is offering here. it is an offering, but a challenging one. The Hebrew word for sheep is *rachel*, which at the root of the word means to journey. The sheep in the fold, the 99, represent the religious leaders, quite possibly the whole nation of israel. The problem is that they aren't journeying. They have become comfortable with where they are. Much like the religious systems of today. All of the religious systems of today. The idea of journeying once again after staying in a place you have come to know so well can be scary, because you have to leave behind many of things you accumulated during your stay. I think this is what happened, the religious leaders forgot how to journey. They got stuck in a rut and were okay with where they were. Have we done the same? Personally? As a community? As humanity?

Jesus is also saying to them that they aren't being who they are meant to be. But even more subversive, He is telling them to be more like the lost sheep. To get lost. Why? Because then they are journeying. And in the act of being lost they are found. That they could learn something from the lost one. Jesus also promises that He will go and find them. Now, a parable that typically gets categorized as a story about redemption is now looked at as a story of redemption in a whole new light of the word. Jesus is inviting us to lose our ways of thinking that create outsiders. It is also saying that the outsider has something to teach us. Maybe redemption isn't about getting saved from something, but learning how to get lost in something. Maybe redemption is losing it all to find what it truly means to be redeemed.

In this context, Jesus continues on with the theme of the lost ones. The next story is the lost coin. And then the story after is one of the most famous stories that has been interpreted and reinterpreted many times over. I would say that the titles that were given to the stories really take away from the power and the depth of all the stories. The writers weren't intending a one-dimensional worldview to be framed out of reading such parables. The nature of a parable is that it leaves room for many interpretations, as does most of the Bible. And so the story of the Prodigal Son when placed back into the whole of the narrative tells a story not of those who are lost, but tells the story of those who need to learn what it means to become lost. To lose all their assumptions about God, the world, scripture, truth and many more things we have accumulated in our 2,000 year sojourn to find true redemption. The traditional definition of redemption is being saved from sin into a new life. According to these short stories, redemption is losing everything. Redemption is the ability to take our cues from the lost. The older son in the story of the Prodigal son who represents the religious elite never came to their senses like the 'lost son' did. There is more to be learned from the lost than we will allow ourselves. The fear is we may go too far. That we might not get found. But maybe that's the wrong assumption because the running threads in this set of 'lost' stories are that those who were lost become found. We have to first be fully lost before being fully found. Peter also asked 'how far is too far?' to Jesus when he inquired about quantitative forgiveness[31]. He wanted to know how much was enough to just get by. Peter was more concerned with how he would look, how his reputation would be tainted in the community. And Jesus responds with numerical metaphor, seventy times seven. Its numerology with a purpose. Seventy is used to describe perfection and seven describes completion and alludes to God's completed act of creation. It's as if Peter was asking 'how far do I need to go to be seen as person who forgives? Or how far is too far? and Jesus responds by telling Peter 'that's the wrong question, just forgive. And when you forgive its as if you helped restore God's creation back to the state it was intended.

figs and the church.

Jesus is walking down the dusty streets with some of his friends and spots this fig tree not bearing fruit. Jesus curses it to never reproduce again and it seems a bit odd to the disciples why Jesus does this. Let me explain. Every State in the USA has a flag that characteristically symbolizes that State's ambience and attitude. For example, California has the Brown Bear as it's emblem of choice which is a symbol of the strength of California. Which was used during the Bear Flag Revolt of 1846 during the Mexican-American War [32.] It was a logo that represented something more, something larger. In this instance, the fig was the country logo for the nation and people of Israel. And Jesus curses the tree? Yep. One characteristic of any fig tree is that you can see its fruit from distance before you even see the leaves. Jesus from way off can see this tree isn't bearing fruit, isn't being what it was meant to be and essentially kills the tree. He is basically saying that Israel as a movement of people has become dead to Him. Of no use. Powerful provocative imagery. You might think I am overstating my case, but in this context of verses Jesus moves on to the temple and in one of his most famous scenes ever recorded he flips the tables and says this, "...is it not written, My house shall be called of all nations the house of prayer but you have made it a den of thieves[33]". Now what was going on here was that the poor were being oppressed. Doves were the bird of choice for the outsider, the unclean and the cripple. Some of the merchants, including the religious leaders would come and take these animals reserved for the unclean and use them for their own financial gain. Jesus was basically calling them self-indulgent. That they somehow learned how to manipulate their cultural knowledge to get something out of it, rather than put something back into it. The phrase "for all nations" would have reminded Jesus' audience of God's words to Abraham. 18 When God chose Abraham he told him that he would be this sort of paternal figure of the Jewish people, not mankind. Some use Abraham as the father of humanity. God didn't say that. He was telling Abraham that he would be a patriarch of the Jewish people. We could too easily take these words and mistake the ethnic for the universal here. As crucial as Abraham is, he is not the 'father' of Christianity. He is the father of the few not the many. A patriarch for the oppressed. But they just didn't get that they weren't meant to be a small exclusive band of people who kept their message away from the world. They were meant to go into it and participate in the life of the world around them. And they are not doing that. And Jesus was challenging them, trying to wake them up. In fact, Jesus goes a step further and he even calls them names. He calls them thieves. Thieves keep things. They steal things. They devalue things. Jesus is throwing this tantrum to bring this point out loud and clear. They are taking a message for the world and keeping it to themselves. I wonder if we have done the same. I think it would be safe to say that we have a habit of trying to keep the message too close to home when the world is in need. Let me be clear, when I say message I don't mean talking about it. I mean living it out. When Jesus uses the word gospel it connotes action. In fact, the word baptism in Jesus' famous last words does not mean to dunk someone in a tank. it is actually the only time where it means action. And so does making disciples; the word for disciple is *talmidim*, an action oriented word. Jesus is saying when you meet up with people, demonstrate this new way of life in the name of the Father, the Son and the Holy Spirit. Also, it is saying that when we demonstrate love and compassion and grace and peace, God is there with us. An amazing reminder that we are not alone in this. That God is here with us every step of the way. Sometimes, I think we can't hear this enough.

Commercials, Articles, and Becoming

By letting it go it all gets done. The world is won by those who let it go. But when you try and try. The world is beyond the winning.
- Lao Tzu

I have noticed more and more magazines that are inundated with commercials and less relevant articles. If you take a closer look at what these one-page eye candy advertisements are selling you might be surprised to know that it is much more than just a product. They are selling you an identity. They are selling you the lie that you may not be good enough without their next big thing. That somehow if you buy 'this one thing', not only will your life be changed but somehow people will like you more and your soul will be at peace. It might sound like I am overstating my case but even Edwin Land who was known for his entrepreneurial prowess said this about marketing, "Marketing is what you do when your product is no good". So, how does knowing this help us find out who we are? I think it's imperative that we know the origin of the messages that we receive on a daily basis, where they come from and if they have any validity at all. The church is one such place. Most of the attempts to evangelise people are really no different from marketing techniques. For the most part, the message of Jesus is nothing more than trying to sell people an identity. Some people run their Jesus campaigns with the urgency of a house on fire and without knowing it turn people and the message into nothing more than cheap trophies we show off on our walls. Yet, the message of Jesus was more about the person and less about the message. Let's dive into another example, like the message of sin. Can we agree that sin is both more and less than missing the mark? That it is also broken relationships between one another. Between us and creation. Between who we are and who we are meant to be. Between the truths we fight for and the lies we can't seem to shake. The Apostle Paul said that it is the "sin" within him, but not him, which seems to be in control. Paul is distinctly separating his identity from sin in and of itself. We are not the sum of our mistakes, bad choices and screw-ups. The word sin isn't as dark and macabre as some of our destructive overtones and church history has led us to believe. In fact, the general Jewish view is that God sees mankind as capable of carrying his message to everyone, everywhere.

So when we are hearing Jesus say "your sins are forgiven[34]" he isn't talking about some "cancerous" disease coursing through our souls. He is defiantly agreeing that he sees more in those people, and he sees more in us. That their actions are not the best them they could be. That there is more to them. In fact the word *chait* is the Hebrew word for sin, which means "not to reach the destination." Sin, in the Hebrew mind, is something that is singular. It is one act, not something that is wrong with being human. It is something we chose to be a part of willingly. If our humanity is the issue then Jesus wouldn't have become human. Humanity isn't the enemy, the orthodox theology about our humanity is.

The story of Adam and Eve is one of the most popular stories of all time; it is also one of the most hijacked stories in the Church. Some ancient theologians thought the story was about sin and how depraved all of creation was. Since then, there are many other opinions on the story. Psychologist Sigmund Freud posited that the Adam and Eve experience was more about maturity and learning, and that all decisions have a direct cause-and-effect clause invisibly attached. And so, what we have is a story of two teenagers who are learning what it is to make beneficial decisions, even ones that might hurt. And the fruit is the metaphor for the process of making and learning self-sacrificing decisions. Freud goes on to say: "The process of maturation occurring in the incidents around the tree describes, in an abstract way, the splitting of the human consciousness into the limited context of conscious thought and the underlying all-aware unconscious[34]."

There are some within the New Age movement who would say that the story is about enlightenment, but also about an intro-duction into dualistic thinking. And so the story about the Fall of Man becomes about how we lost the awareness that we were always connected with the divine. And so then, in that instance, sin becomes about accepting dualism as reality and about how we are somehow permanently disconnected from God.

I think Christians may have to accept that sin isn't the reason why we're frail. That frailty isn't even an enemy. That frailty is simply on the journey with us. To teach us, hold us, cry with us. And to transform us into whom we are meant to be. This last point is important to understand because "sin" isn't patho-logical. The word directly refers to personal potential. And so sin isn't what's inherently wrong with us; it's the process whereby we learn to live out who we are meant to be. It is about how we can grow rather than how we are impeded. It's about who we are becoming rather than who we once were. So what does that do with evil? Let me be clear, evil exists. It is real. It exists when we do nothing in response to global crises. It exists when life is taken. It exists when we intentionally create opportunities for destructive outcomes. Evil can be sin. Sin can also be evil. The issue with the Western idea of sin is when we use it to create the very barriers that Jesus death came to dismantle.

This is an invitation to those who, with the word "sin," would unintentionally but aggressively cheapen our experience of life and the divine within it: maybe we can agree that we might have got it wrong. And that we might have got it wrong for thousands of years. And that's okay, because life is about maturing and moving on and learning to make self-sacrificing decisions. Maybe the best decision we can make now is to let go of what we have been taught to hold onto so tightly.

the world of not enough.
Our society, along with television commercials that parade across our screens compel us to get more. That what we have now is not enough. Yet, there are those who are born into the world of "not enough" and we still think it right to desire more, more and more. This desire to want more while others have less is sin. It is something that can be reversed. When Jesus defends the women caught in adultery and challenges her to "go and (do this) sin no more", he is essentially saying, "you are above that", "you are better than this". Jesus is encouraging her to live to her full potential. It's grasping the divine commerce that giving is the new receiving. It is in the giving of ourselves that we find more of who we are meant to be. Jesus said it this way, "If anyone follows me, he must deny himself''. Jesus says the way to find ourselves is giving it all up. It's as if one of the most divine acts we can participate in is 'having nothing' for the benefit of humanity. Jesus comes in and just dismantles the whole system of becoming clean by saying that there is more to them than what they think of themselves and there is more to them than the Pharisees think of them. This would frustrate anyone who created a list of purification rules. We are more than a list of rules. We have always been more.

Our identity rests in the fact that we have been fully redeemed. Now, I am not one for churchy words, but a little history about redemption before we go on.

redemption defined.
The Jewish people were oppressed by the Egyptian ruler Pharaoh who was quite ruthless in his dealing with slaves. For sport, Pharaoh would force the Jewish slaves to hunt wild beasts, regardless of the outcome. He would stone them if they didn't produce enough bricks. He would keep them working past midnight and beyond. If you notice, each plague corresponds with the act of mistreatment at the hand of one of its cruelest

rulers. Then they cried out. This is where redemption started. A realization that they were in need. An open awareness of their oppressed state. God responded through Moses and began the process of redeeming Her people. God tends to respond with people, not theology. God responds with Abraham, then with Moses, then with Joshua, then with David and then with Jesus. So redemption is less about the words we use and more about how we respond to the other. Redemption is an act not a prayer. Redemption is being the answer to the prayer. *Padah* is the Hebrew word for redemption, the idea behind the word paints the picture of someone being freed or untied from any kind of bondage or slavery. In this definition there is no requirement for any specific method of redemption. The act of redemption is the point, not how they are freed. In Christianity, there is this aggressive tendency to try and define redemption through certain methodology. Some believe to be redeemed we need to say what some have called the 'sinners prayer', which is a prayer of confession and repentance. Others believe we are still being redeemed. All of these views are hidden behind the assumption that Jesus came to die for our sins. But, as I have said before, maybe sin wasn't why He came. The act of salvation wasn't necessarily about our sin, it was the Son of God coming to show us what it looks like when we die to ourselves and invest ourselves in the other, the stranger, the friend, and the person in need. Maybe Christ's death was also to show us that oppression doesn't have the last word, but love does. That love is the new redemption. That love changes everything. That dying to ourselves is the only way we can bring in resurrection.

the backdoor of heaven.
It took the whole of the Old Testament for the Jewish Egyptian slaves under Pharaoh's hand to find out what it looks like not to be slaves. They had gotten used it. They somehow believed the lie that they were nothing more than slaves. They watched the

commercial and believed the advertisement. In fact, when times got hard, they preferred slavery over their new found freedom.

As exciting as it is, it can be immobilizing if you have never known the experience of letting go. Like the Israelites freed from slavery, letting go leaves us naked and cold. We find safety and warmth in what we know. Our identity is formed by what we know rather than what we don't know. Knowledge has somehow become our saviour. And that saviour is a fair-weather friend. Because if we base the very essence of who we are on knowledge (e.g., theology, bibliology, eschatology and etc.) when we don't arrive at an answer, we then come to believe the lie that we are nothing. We become the very things we believe. Becoming slaves to knowledge gives us the illusion that we are powerful, influential and that we somehow have tapped into the secret backdoor of heaven. That the more we know the more God is attracted to us. I used to think this way growing up; I used to write down bible verses and test myself and even tried to become the Steven Hawking of biblical knowledge. But, if I can be completely honest, it was so exhausting! I remember hiking through the mountains a few years back and having a conversation with God, more like yelling at Him for not having my life in order (*back when I thought that was his main responsibility!*). In a moment of miraculous silence, as I was walking off the beaten path and studying the rocks as they each passed by me, it was if God had reached into me and whispered, "I just want to enjoy the rocks with you!" That's all I heard. That's all I needed to hear. It was a turning point in my life. I realized that I needed to be silent more and that in that contemplation the holy divine responded. This isn't some full proof way to get God respond. To be honest, I think sometimes we focus way too much on figuring that out. I think like the author of Ecclesiastes who says "God has set eternity into the hearts of men[36]." It's inside of us, rather than outside of us.

playing artfully in the dirt.

I have shared life with many Christian communities around the globe, and my experience with these communities is that they spend a lot of time on the subject of sin and sin management. I walked into a non-denominational church in India a few years ago, the pastor was preaching in broken English, quite well actually. A few sentences into his sermon he began to talk how the world and our humanity are utterly depraved, almost to the point of sheer uselessness without God.

That message forced a question out of me that I am still asking, "how does this kind of message instil hope, grace, peace, redemption and love?" Where in that message is the message that God sees humanity as partners, not as enemies. We will talk about this more in future chapters.

What I have noticed is that the narrative arc in the New Testament contradicts a lot of what seems to be a universal message of sadness that has been perpetuated for centuries. Follow me. A woman who might have been in her late teens was caught in the act of adultery, practically stripped bare and thrown at the feet of Jesus as a test. She is a woman in a culture where women are colonized as property. She was also a woman with a really bad reputation who was caught in an act that made her even more unclean and rejectable to those in her society. But, the guy involved was nowhere on the scene. According to the Torah law, both would have been stoned to death on the spot. The group of religious leaders began challenging Jesus in their expected Jewish manner, typically by either leading a conversation through questions or by quoting their tribal prophet. Now, what it's significant to notice here, is that in a community of people who do not separate their beliefs from their everyday life, to them the tribal prophet was the ultimate authority. No one is supposed to question the tribal prophet. No one. Yet, Jesus goes on to respond by playing artfully in the dirt. Dirt in that culture, well, was dirty. You were unclean if you touched it. By playing connect the dots in the dirt Jesus equates himself to the woman at his feet. He was also challenging the tribal prophet and essentially saying that He was bigger than their tribe. He was bigger than a denomination or even Christianity. Then he turns and responds to the woman who is still crying and expecting judgment and tells her to live her life differently. Why? Because she has met Jesus who believes she can. The famous phrase slips off of the Teacher's lips, dripped in so much grace that there was no room for condemnation or judging. "Go and sin no more"[37]. The word for sin that Jesus uses here is one that speaks of sin as something temporary and in the moment. In fact the Hebrew word for sin is pronounced *khate*. It means that sin isn't a forever kind of thing. it isn't an act that continues. In fact, Judaism says that sin is an act, not a state of being. That we can all participate in the ways of sin. We can oppress one another. We can hurt each other and God. Remember, Christianity was birthed out of Judaism. Jesus practiced Jewish holidays, customs and challenged the ones that separated those in need. If sin is not a state of being, then where did we go wrong? Have we been reading scripture through another lens that may limit our insight?

orthodox atonement.
The orthodox view of atonement, which I have and will continue to deal with throughout the book, is quite pervasive theology that seems to unintentionally remove the influence behind the purposes of why Jesus might have died as an example to humanity. At this point in the story, I am going to deal with it as if I agree with it. Let's start with the idea of depravity.

Can we agree that all of creation has been restored and is being restored? If so, this means we no longer have to spend so much of our time focusing on how depraved and evil we could be, rather we can begin asking the question post-sin, post-cross, and post-tomb: "What does it look like to be Christ in everything

I say and do?" or "What does it mean to be Christ to the outsider?" Maybe even a better one is, "what does it mean for me to live out the best me that God intended?" These are the questions we should be expending ourselves over. Not "how sinful am I?" In this theory, that assumes the cross just wasn't good enough. Also, the danger is we can be focusing on a problem that has already been relinquished on the cross. A problem that by its own nature is dead because it has been killed. Why would we intentionally focus on something destructive when God himself sees us all as already forgiven? Some of the authors in scripture believed that Jesus came to fix everything. To heal everyone in this world. They called the problem he came to die for 'sin'. This is just one interpretation. One, not the only right one. And if their worldview has validity, listen to what one of its followers had to say, the author of Hebrews says this "And by that will we have been sanctified through the offering of the body of Jesus Christ once for all[38]."Whether someone chooses that forgiveness is a whole different subject entirely). I think we might have a hard time believing that God's forgiveness is either good enough or whether it's even true. We have done what Blaise Pascal said we would do: "God made man in his image, and we returned the favor". We have designed a God who has limits on his grace. Sure, we won't admit that in theory. But the way we live life and the way we tend to communicate with God and others demonstrates how we see God and truth. And I believe most of us, because of what and how we have been taught, have a hard time accepting that God's grace truly covers everything. But, according to God—it does. We are no longer sinners. Once we realize this, I think we can move forward. I think God is a fan of forward motion and progress. This new-found identity then leads us into a community of people who look outwards. Focusing on ourselves deprives those in need of something deeper than simply food or shelter. It deprives them of the human connection.

homosexuals, pastors, and samaritans.

The story of the Good Samaritan not only teaches us about the other but also about plurality. Not just religious plurality but also a theory of leadership plurality[39]. The ability to have alternative leadership within churches. One of the things that the story could teach us is that all people have a purpose and that there should even be homosexual pastors who can add to the conversation. If we have learned anything thus far its that God chooses who has something to say, not man. The moment we define who God chooses to use, is the moment God stops being God and starts being a god. Homosexuality teaches us that there is a need to embrace diversity[40]. That diversity is a God-given feature within each of us. That plurality exists not only in leadership but as a lens with which to see the world. The more Christians spend their time pointing the finger, the less time we spend trying to find ways to work together to heal the brokenness in the world around us. It just seems that Jesus was more concerned about bringing peace into the relationships within humanity. He talks a lot about love, forgiveness, and embracing the outsider. If the Church has made the homosexual community an outsider and Jesus is for the outsider, shouldn't we be following Him rather than our versions of Him?

Why do we feel the need to still judge people and stand at a safe distance from those who live "different" lives, or to use a more fundamental word, those who live "sinful" ways of life? Some people might say that they have moved passed judging others, but what is your initial reaction when you meet a person who has been "painted" a sinner? When we feel the need to judge others based on our own versions of specified criterion we have taken all of our inadequacies and fears and allowed them to be king for the day. I think for us, it is a lot easier to see someone else's faults before admitting our own. Maybe we are supposed to continually revisit our own actions and attitudes in light of others and especially in light of the reality that all of creation is truly part of the new creation initiated by the cross. When we take the time to revisit and if necessary reinterpret what we say we believe than as a global family we can all come together and discover in harmony who God has meant us to be. What if we look at the words of Jesus as a metaphor for our individual and global potential? Theopoetics is a strand in philosophy that seeks to look at God, the Bible and concepts of truth as metaphors for the bigger picture. Activist and non-violence trainer Matt Guynn says this about the art of Theopoetics "The task of the theopoetic and the theopoet is to open up spaces of unanticipated dreaming in which the past, the present and the future are reshaped as we reorganize or even recreate our stories in relationship with the other, the world and the Divine[41]." It applies the assumption that things like metaphor, myth, and story are intrinsically valuable to our development as people. Let's take for example the words of Jesus in John where He says "I and the Father are one"[42]. Jesus and God were in sync with one another, they had a relationship like lovers do. But even more than that Jesus was saying He was God. Jesus was claiming divinity. And he doesn't end there, He says we could be just like Him. We too can be God in the flesh. Not that we are God in his fullness, but that we are all connected to the divine. This isn't such a crazy claim to those in the Eastern religions including Judaism, they all believed everything is connected, even now. Jesus prayed that we could all be one, which is also the same word that signified Jesus' symbiotic connection to the divine. *Theopoetics* might say that Jesus didn't just utter these words for his own benefit, he also said them because its who we could also become. That his relationship with God is a metaphor for our relationship with God.

like lovers do.

There's a lot of romantic language that we sometimes miss in scripture when we read it literally. Sometimes reading it literally strips the context of it poetic nature, like the words Jesus chose above about his relationship with God. The word for one has erotic implications. It is the deepest of all metaphors. It is the realization that language has its limits and Jesus was sharing that here. So when our language doesn't say what we mean, we turn to poetry or song to tell others of how we feel[43].

Cigar-toting South American poet Pablo Neruda had this notorious quirky ability to compose quite metaphorically creative poems. Neruda wrote this poem for one of his many lovers, and it we peer deep enough we might find the language that Jesus was trying to use.

"I do not love you as if you were salt-rose, or topaz,
or the arrow of carnations the fire shoots off.
I love you as certain dark things are to be loved,
in secret, between the shadow and the soul.

I love you as the plant that never blooms
but carries in itself the light of hidden flowers;
thanks to your love a certain solid fragrance,
risen from the earth, lives darkly in my body.

I love you without knowing how, or when, or from where.
I love you as straightforwardly, without complexities or pride;
so I love you because I know no other way

than this: where I does not exist, nor you,
so close that your hand on my chest is my hand,
so close that your eyes close as I fall asleep."

These words are the words that might have dripped from the lips of Jesus to God, if he were poet. They were so close they were able to finish each others sentences. This is so much more prominent than simple candle-light dinners. He came here to demonstrate what we can have with God. Not when He returns.

Not one day when. Now. This moment. While you are reading this, you were made to be 'one' with God. Jesus knew God and was one with him. The word know in Hebrew is a sexual term. When scripture states that Adam *knew* Eve, it didn't mean he knew her date of birth or ring size. Nope. Adam *knew* Eve. I believe this is an integral part of our existence and we can't simplify it by being politically correct. This is a scandalous metaphor for oneness with our Creator.

the movie life.
I believe if a lot of the religious mystics were alive today they would be movie producers. Movies are one of the greatest metaphors for life. I think we might need to recapture the movie life within. Within church. Within faith. You know those movies that make you cry. Or cringe. Or wish for more. Or make you want to love all over again. Somehow we have to learn how to reintroduce those feelings back into our lives, a much needed pathos. Dreams. Passion. Broken hearts. This is what keeps us going. This is what should drive us and also makes life so much worth living. It's too easy to explain away things as fate or divine intervention. When we use words like providence we end the story before it begins. The mystery dies with the explanation. We need to come to our senses, quite literally and realize that there is a reason we were made to bleed. Made to feel. Made to experience love, loss and all the things in between. Without these things, life is nothing more than a script about a bunch of humanoids that learn life is not about living it here but about someplace out there that is waiting for us to die. This theology or minimizing of life takes away the meaning of a first kiss, of a broken heart, of a grandmother who has recently passed, or the first bicycle waiting for you to ride it down the block. Life is this amazing adventure that has all these twists and turns, and the scandal of mystery brings that back to us. We need mystery to return again and again to remind us that life is about love not

theology. That love is the study of God. I have met many Christians, along with being one of them, who at times were so nervous and stagnated by the possibility of getting it all wrong. If God is love, then He is love. If He is not, then we should end the book here. I struggle with a God who is not compelled by love but what I have done wrong. I think He might only exist in our educational processes of trying to figure Him out. If God is love and He made us to emulate Him, and then wouldn't it make sense that He might desire for us to stay around and demonstrate that kind of love in inventive ways? It seems that Jesus didn't come here to make us ready for some big day in some golden city. Sure there are apparent inclinations to read scripture in such a light. Why not? It makes us feel good and gives us something to look forward to right? I am not saying that there won't be a day when we meet up with our Creator, but God comes here. The City spoken of in the book of Revelation descends from heaven[44]. I am sure that those details will play themselves out one day in God's own time. Christ's relationship with God is an invitation to have the same kind of symbiotic rhythm that they had. The mystics caught on to this. The prophets did too. They had such intense belief that they could have what they called "Union with God". In fact, St.Teresa of Avila, the mother of Christian mysticism said this: "Take God for your spouse and friend and walk with Him continually, and you will not sin, will learn to love, and the things you must do will work out prosperously for you." It is this kind of language that evokes the imagination of a couple who are so in love that they don't know what it's like to be without one another. Teresa of Avila figured out that the love that is shared with God also comes with this intense desire to work together. To build and create. To inspire and move forward. It is this that we should seek. It is this very thing we should crave. It's no surprise that Jesus used words like freedom. At times we are the ones with our ideas and theologies that get in the way of that liberation. I think this is because we are afraid of what it means to be free. At one of his speeches, Nelson Mandela quotes guru Marianne Williamson who once said: "Our deepest fear is not that we are inadequate. Our deepest fear is that we are powerful beyond measure. It is our light, not our darkness that most frightens us." Jesus says it another way, "...you are the light of the world...". Later, a few chapters away He is talking to a crowd of people and Jesus tells them: "...I am the light of the world..." If you take these two phrases at face value, Jesus is saying that we have it in us to be a community of people who can extinguish dark things. And when we extinguish those dark things its as if we are incarnating Her into those dark moments. We have it in us to incarnate hope into hopeless situations, into homeless contexts, into war and into unforgiving places. We are the light. If we accept who we are then we too can change societies, reinvent politics, change cultures, transform the lives of those on the margins and embrace the liberation He came to give us all. Jesus came to show us a new kind of humanity. A humanity where mankind embraces the divine within and learns to live it out in such a way that political powers begin taking cues from us. That societies begin looking outward rather than inward. A world that sees everything as a gift.

Breathe in. Breathe out. That is a gift. And God revels in each of us as the greatest gift He gave Himself. At our creation, the Creator was lost for words. We were "very good" or really beautiful might be a better rendering. We still are. That doesn't change. God's jaw dropped when he saw you and I. His jaw still drops when new life is ushered into the world. This kind of God we most of the time miss, because there is a tendency to either focus, or in the name of balance try to bring in, a God who solely expends himself in anger over what we do or don't do.

theology is insufficient.
We have been talking a lot about the inadequacies of theology, why? Why do I keep talking on this subject? It seems because

Christians have come to a place where we think theology has this saving power to it, and that theology has all the answers. Yet, the Bible says something entirely different. In scripture, the prophet Isaiah catches on to this idea that God is beyond human cognition. That He is not the sum of our theology or even our interpretations of scripture. In fact, we need to bury theology 6 feet deep. At one time, the term meant *'words about God'*, but unfortunately now has gotten in the way of God. We need something new. Theology as is is insufficient. This is why contemplation is significant; it gives God a chance to speak on God. Maybe we can adopt theological non-cognitivism[45] as a new approach to experiencing the enigmatic divine that is God. This atheistic approach states that words are useless when talking about the divine. It even goes a step further and says that words about God don't fully register in our brains, other than being some form of minimalist rhetoric. If we live out a Christ-centred theological non-cognitivism than following in the way of Christ becomes the point of our journey rather than whether we have a right or wrong belief, articles of faith, and truth. Not that they aren't salient but if we release them from being at the centre, it leaves room for the mystery of God to woo us into rediscovery. Maybe we can be a people who are theologically agnostic and allow space for God to blow our presuppositions out of the water. It starts with realizing that She is more. This more is where we start. It's like meeting the person of your dreams and then not being able to find the words to actually translate why your heart is beating a million miles a minute. And then when you do find the words, its being frustrated that they don't quite seem to measure up to the feelings that are raging inside. This is why we need theological non-cognitivism; this hunger for God and who He is will be enough to transform us more than any sermon, any verse memorization, and any bible study or group gathering. As important as these are, they should not be the point. God desires more for us, why don't we? What if we are afraid of what God wants to give because we are happy where we are? We are comfortable with who we have become. Because our comfort seems sitting on the throne, our identity doesn't rest in God alone. It finds rest in a small God who bends to our every whim. Because we don't know what to do with our questions and doubts, our identity is what suffers. So, instead of asking questions, we become mesmerized by someone behind a pulpit who has the ability to dazzle us with words (who knows. I am may be dazzling you now) and either makes us feel guilty or good about the questions that inhabit us.

the art of metaphor.

The ancient Rabbis had this art, no responsibility, to see beyond scripture. They had this knack for taking a story (whether it was true or not) and finding deeper meaning rather than what was right before their eyes. It would be like dipping your hand in a lake not knowing what you might get and you end up grabbing a handful of pearls. According to an online source, "The ford of the river Jabbok was the place where there was a conflict between two paths. It was at the confluence between two streams. It was also the only place where it was possible to brave and wade through the torrent that crossed the path of the road or trek that passed on further into the land of Israel. At certain times of year this was quite a struggle, and especially if there were goods to be carried over, cattle and flocks to be got across, not to mention family and children[46]"... This was the nearest river Jacob camped at, where the infamous first recorded wrestling match occurred. The Rabbis wouldn't have just seen this as one of their ancient brothers in a battle with God. They might have it seen it as a metaphor that to be a Jew is to wrestle. To be a person who follows God, is to wrestle. Grapple with questions, doubts and fears. Maybe some, who go to church and get told that doubt is wrong, walk away disheartened by the untruth that has just been shared. Then they go home and try their hardest not to struggle, not to doubt, not to question — yet they do. Riddled with guilt.

Well my friend, you are in good company with these ancient wanderers.

ancient wanderers.

When we meet up with Jacob, he isn't comfortable with who He is. He uses his brother's name Esau, for starters. Then years pass and we meet up with him again and he finally gets to a place where he is comfortable in his skin. He accepts who he is. And then in great Jewish humor fashion; God changes his name. Can we all agree that there is something beautiful about coming into who we were meant to be? Finding that we are so much more than we are now. That God believes we have it in us to be like Him. So much so He signed on the dotted line when He created us, and somewhere in our souls it says "authentic copy, one of a kind". This God wants you to know that you are on your way...

The Conflicted Tortoise

Don't be afraid of opposition. Remember, a kite rises against; not with the wind.
— Hamilton Mabie

I think we need conflict. I have had a difficult time debating this issue with myself or whether I should even write this chapter. I hate conflict, and I hate fights. I care about what people think of me way too much. In fact, on a gut level, I want to think that conflict is useless. At least, due to my childhood experiences, I have come to believe that conflict can only be destructive and never formational. Our family living room was a war zone that somehow emulated scenes from an episode of Jerry Springer. He screams at her, she throws things at him, he runs out the door and the cycle replays itself over and over. So, my throat has a big lumpy gulp stuck right in the middle of my throat just knowing where this conversation is going to lead.

There is a familiar story that has been floating around now for centuries. It has even showed up in our cartoon mythology. It's the story of a hopeless Tortoise who just cannot seem to get it together and a Hare who seems to know all the tricks of the path. As the story goes, the Hare challenges the Tortoise to a race. During the race however, the Hare thinks so highly of himself that he decides to take a nap. And in that time, the Tortoise discovers his potential. Now, depending on what cartoon you saw when you were little, the Tortoise might have simply won the race because he tried so hard. The one that has been embedded in my mind is the one where the Tortoise stretches his neck out and uses a part of himself that he was never aware of to win the race and win the gold. Conflict brings potential. Adversity brings pain. Pain brings change. Change affects the world. I know you might be thinking that this might be

81

overstating my case a bit, after all this was a short story written by a famous slave who lived within a society who endorsed conflict. Late psychologist M. Scott Peck said this about conflict: "The truth is that our finest moments are most likely to occur when we are feeling deeply uncomfortable, unhappy, or unfulfilled. For it is only in such moments, propelled by our discomfort, that we are likely to step out of our ruts and start searching for different ways or truer answers."

Conflict isn't justification for global chaos. War is destructive. Do we ever need war? If we ask that question then we should also ask the following questions: Do we need unnecessary death? Do we need governmental oppression? Do we need justified evil behavior?[47] Like Gandhi once said: "You can't shake hands with a clenched fist." If we condone acts of war then we also help pull the trigger. If we fall victim to our nationalistic approaches to war that seem to be founded upon subjective views of personal ethics, than we demean humanity to nothing more than pawns on a chess board. Life then becomes something we gamble with rather than something we uphold. The words of Jesus that show up the most in scripture are shalom and love. Why? To make a point that life is lived well when it is lived in harmony. Yet, there is also a harmony within regenerative conflict. It is the conflict we experience in life that helps mold us into who we are and can become. In the West, we have been conditioned to think that pain and conflict should be avoided. Words like pain tend to fall in the category of "things not to talk about." This is an after-effect of our culture of denial that tells us what we should and shouldn't be talking about. Yet, think back to those times of personal conflict, and sure, they were not the most exciting times in your life but what was gained in such painful moments has now helped you become who you were meant to be.

graphic provocative imagery.
Jesus is talking with a bunch of his friends and He challenges

them to think about what they are getting themselves into by choosing to follow Him. Then he goes into graphic provocative imagery of what their lives might look like if they commit themselves to the cause. Then he said to them all: "If anyone would come after me, he must deny himself and take up his cross daily and follow me". To understand what Jesus was saying, I think we have to go back to the cross. The cross was much like our electric chair, but it was messier in the aftermath. It was an instrument designed to publicly humiliate the criminal that hung on it. They would usually start by whipping them with a cat-o-nine tails which had shards of rocks and bones to strip the flesh. The Roman government would also require them to be naked. There were no laws of public indecency in the time of Roman rule, in fact, they loved the human body. The Roman population learned most of their love of the human body from their Greek neighbors. Historians go on to say that the cross was all about lowering the status of those who were being hung. We could go on and on, but there are enough good books on this subject already. Jesus was not using mythical language here. He was talking about us taking up our own cross and following him.

ground zero.

The Aramaic word for death is *Mowth*, it means, well, death. Unfortunately, Jesus wasn't sugar-coating this phrase by using rich Hebrew imagery. He was using the violent death of the cross as a metaphor for a way of life. Death into life. Death equals life. Giving up for the benefit of another is life. A paradox of opposites. Letting go of things that slow us down equals life. Conflict is a sort of death we each have to go through to become more of who we are meant to be.

Braveheart is one of my favorite movies of all time. Let's forget the historical absurdities for a moment and embrace the movie for what it is - a good story. It tells the story of an average man who by a series of unfortunate events becomes a hero of freedom for his people. Towards the end of the movie, William Wallace is having a conversation with the Princess Isabelle and she is attempting to persuade William to save his own life. He responds, "All men die, few men truly live." This was a man who was ready to die. He learned to see conflict as something we go through to make transformative changes. He was in touch with the reality that in just a few moments, his life would be over. He would stop breathing. But his legacy would go on. Most heroic people are in touch with their own mortality. They realize their lives aren't the point, that they are a part of something paramount. They are not afraid of death. But for some reason, our culture is. We have come to believe that death has the last word. This is another tell-tell sign that dualism is telling us how we should see the world. If you have a moment go turn on the television and count how many commercials have to do with ageing and other products that are being sold to preserve our youth. The amount is ludicrous. We do not talk about it, because we're afraid of it. But like any conflict, to deal with it, we have to go through it with one another. We need to talk about it. Accept it as a reality. Say it with me "We are all going to die one day". It's not a comforting thing to confess, I get it. I have trouble proclaiming that reality too. I am learning with you. Conflict is the same. No one is excited talking about conflict. We would rather presume everything is alright, when deep down we know things are actually falling apart. So, we need heroes who are going to stand in the gap. Stand in the silence and say something. So when Jesus invites the disciples to take up their cross, He is inviting them into an heroic way of living. That they too must come to terms with the fact that their lives are a part of something bigger. Jesus somehow believed His way of life could actually change the world. And so did those who followed Him. Jesus is saying that it is in our conflict[48], our times of hardship that we find our dreams. Jesus then says we must "deny ourselves". It almost sounds like he is giving a depressing eulogy before we are even pushing up daisies. What if that's not what he was saying though? The word for *deny* in the Aramaic is the same English word for *contradict*. Again, at the heart of contradiction is conflict. If we're given choices to make and we choose one object over the other we are essentially agreeing with the idea that our choice was better than all the others. On a personal level Jesus is appealing to our better selves and is challenging us all to intentionally choose the better us. At times, we must be willing to make decisions for the greater good that may cost us everything. What if we change the cross with the word cause? What is your cause? Why are you here? Are you here to follow Jesus? To follow Buddha? Money? Happiness? Take whatever your cause is and replace it with the cross in that verse. Jesus wants us to see that we must be ready to die for what we believe in[49] Not the kind of death that involves killing others for the cause or physically dying for ours. Maybe a better way of describing this idea of dying for something would be to use the phrase self-denial. So maybe a new rendering or way to see the verse would be to say that there are moments in life where we might need to boycott our selfish inclinations and abandon them for the greater good. This is why personal conflict is essential; it is the mirror that shows us what we need to give up finding the us that we are meant to be. Some of you may be reading this and have a hard time with this as a conversation topic. I understand. I too am having a hard time writing this as a person who grew up in a conflict-ridden living room. I don't want to cheapen your own experience of conflict. If anything I want to validate it and point it out as something that might have been unfair and painful and to remind you it is not your fault. But also at ground zero, years later, it too can be something we could learn from. But, what if our life experiences have taught us only one side to the benefits of conflict? What if we have become victims of our childhood and environment and they have created this fear of conflict? If this is you, it is important to deal with these issues head-on. It is imperative that we, especially as Westerners, come to terms with the healthy side of conflict. Whatever that means for you, look for healing. For me, It means counseling and dealing with my demons that are sometimes too easy to hide behind my Sunday smiles.

living in the same room.

In the book of Lamentations[50], there is a story of Israel going through a heap of conflict. Historical conflict, geographical, national, and personal. Just to name a few. The story is written in the descriptive style of a Hebrew poem. Here's the backdrop. Israel is personified as a woman who is in utter pain and experiencing conflict. There is also a pedestrian narrator who looks on. Then there is a *gibbor* or "mighty man", maybe a closer rendering from the Hebrew would be "hero". This gibbor starts out like more of a reporter who is chronicling events in the life of Israel. Then in Chapter 3, everything shifts. He feels her pain. He even uses graphic imagery to describe the emotional violence he is experiencing just watching this go on. Have you ever turned on your television and watched so much agony that you felt like you had to turn away? Have you ever experienced so much pain that all you felt like doing was running from the atrocious scene? This is what's going on here. "The LORD filled me with misery; he made me drunk with suffering. He broke my teeth with gravel and trampled me into the dirt. I have no more peace." Here is a man who has seen so much pain in another that he is actually questioning whether he wants to be alive. Yet later he says "...the Lord is my portion." What? He literally bears his soul and practically rails against God and then comes up with the conclusion that God is more than enough? If I was Jeremiah, I am not sure I would be writing those words in the same sentence. Then again, if I was Jeremiah, I might not have a problem with hope and despair being bedfellows. In the West, hope is typically defined as something we get or experience post-despair. Even our cliches allude to this way of thinking. "The sun shines *after* the rain". More often than not, it seems that David is angry at God for abandoning him and leaving him for dead. You ever feel like that about God? David did. But then he tends to come to the apparent conclusion that "God is good".

Yes, David too came to the same conclusion that the author of Lamentations did. That hope and despair can live in the same room together. We are taught that we should not talk about certain things in our culture. This culture of denial has led us to believe that everything we say and do and live has its own little compartment that it should stay in. Even hope and despair. But without despair, you don't need hope. Without hope, all you would have is despair. They need one another. So does conflict. Without peace, all you would ever know is conflict. But without conflict, you don't need peace. We need conflict to remind us of peace. To remind us why we're here. Now, I don't think that means you need to put this book down and go to look for conflict. But, I think we have learned to run from the very thing we need to help make us who we are meant to be. Go ahead and daydream about a moment, either recent or in the past, where you experienced some sort of deep tension. How did it make you feel? Where were you? Why were you there? Now, ask yourself: "What did learn from this experience? How did it make me a better person?" Now when I use the word conflict or tension, I do not mean when someone is raped or beaten or abused. We are not talking about someone else's destructive choices and how they may have shaped you. However, these choices are important and need to be dealt with. Evil behavior on someone else's part that unfortunately has been placed into your life is not what I mean when I use this idea of conflict. I am so sorry you ever had to deal with that and am grieving with you in your loss. M. Scott Peck said this: "The truth is that our finest moments are most likely to occur when we are feeling deeply uncomfortable, unhappy, or unfulfilled. For it is only in such moments, propelled by our discomfort, that we are likely to step out of our ruts and start searching for different ways or truer answers..." See how, conflict leads to transformation. If the end goal of conflict is to lead to some sort of transformation or change, then we can call that "Transformance Conflict". The Jews believed we need conflict.

If you look at the Old Testament, you will see a small nation formed by conflict. A nation that like us, somehow learned to run and hide from conflict. They didn't want conflict. According to online sources the story goes something like this, "However, in about 930 BC the United Kingdom split, with ten of the twelve Tribes of Israel rejecting Solomon's son Rehoboam as their king. The Tribes of Judah and Benjamin remained loyal to Rehoboam, and reformed the Kingdom of Judah, while the other entity continuing to be called the Kingdom of Israel, or Israel. The Kingdom of Judah is also often referred to as the Southern Kingdom, while the Kingdom of Israel following the split is referred to as the Northern Kingdom. Judah existed until 586 BC, when it was conquered by the Babylonian Empire under Nebuzar-adan, captain of Nebuchadnezzar's body-guard. [2] With the deportation of most of the population and the destruction of the Temple and of Jerusalem, the destruction of the kingdom was complete. Gedaliah, with a Chaldean guard stationed at Mizpah, was made governor to rule over Judah..."

the birth of irresponsibility or satan.

Judah got comfortable with their time in Babylon. They began accepting the Babylonian belief system and mixing it in with theirs. Synchronicity. One major religion in that time was Zoroastrianism. Without going into too much detail here, some of the main creeds of this faith are:

1. *A belief in a place called heaven*
2. *The belief in an ultimate arch-enemy of God called Satan*
3. *A belief in a place of eternal damnation*

As the days went on and the Jews became more synchronized with the belief in Zoroastrianism, they too began believing in some of these things. There were no recorded beliefs within Judaism that claimed the existence of some type of evil-encompassing being who would run around trying to tempt us to destructive ends.That worldview didn't come into play until the New Testament and tends to be used as rhetoric. The term devil doesn't even show up in the Old Testament and the title Satan only appears 19 times and mostly in the story of Job. But, Satan is a servant of God in that story. The Jewish view of Satan defines the term as a thing rather than a person. The word Satan means 'one who opposes' or 'adversary. The ancient Jewish people believed that we needed adversity in our life. They too believed we couldn't become who we were meant to be without conflict. We need conflict. We need Satan. (Now, if you've read this with Western eyes, you just thought of some guy painted all red in a suit with a pitchfork.) Again, this idea of Satan being a person did not come from our ancient pre-Christian roots. It stemmed from a religion that was around the same time that Judaism was still forming itself. To recklessly perpetuate the myth of Satan is to perpetuate a spirit of irresponsibility for one another. By focusing all of our energy on a fabled character and blaming him for all of our struggles and pain is to cheapen our experiences as we journey through life. Pointing the finger at something else or some one else gives our pain purpose, it helps us make sense of all of our struggles. So on one level it makes sense to have the existence of Satan as part of our cosmology. Yet, it is a bad stewardship of acceptance. Like accepting that we can't be always be in control or accepting that our choices affect us and those around us. It might just be easier if we accept that struggle, pain and strife are character building protagonists in our story. That without them, as the ancient Jews believed life would simply be boring. This isn't to trivialize or cheapen anyone's experience of hell on earth; it is to give it even more meaning beyond the typical Christian response. When Peter is told by Jesus to get behind Him and Jesus calls Peter "Satan", Jesus isn't calling him the person we think Satan is, but most likely was referring to Peter as a person who was blocking his path, or someone who was stepping in the way of what He knows He has come to do. We can all be Satan. We can all get in the way of someone's development. Or a better world. Or a better environment. We can either add to the evils or help remove them. Now the Jewish view[51], is that adversity also comes out of God himself. In the poetic myth-story of Job, Satan is a servant of God. We have been talking about how hope lives with despair, conflict resides with peace, and now to add to the mix, adversity comes from God. "I form the light and create darkness, I bring prosperity and create disaster; I, the LORD, do all these things." This is the prophet Isaiah describing the character of God. He is committed to our development, to us becoming more like Him. This verse does not say God is all evil, it does not endorse a theology of God going around creating evil. It does say that He had a hand in forming darkness[52], the absence of light. God forms or shapes the darkness in our life. He has to purposefully create light. Light emanates from God. But he intentionally moulds the darkness and seems to have a purpose in it. That He contributes himself to it. But that we are responsible for how we choose to use it. The Jewish idea of darkness is that we need it to help create distinction. That if light was all by itself, all things would remain the same. There would be no difference. There is also a Jewish story of how light and dark were in conflict with one another and that God created peace between them. Ancient Rabbis said this, " Evil is something that is allowed by God in order that the good should become manifest and known." There is a tendency in our Western approach to think that opposites don't attract. Sure, we believe this in romantic settings, but we tend to reject this in every other environment. It seems impossible that loss can come from the same place as gain. Or that joy can dance with confusion. But this is central to what the origins of our faith teach us. So, where do we go from here? I think it challenges us to let go of our need for explanation. Our need for things to make sense in a linear way. I think part of the change is that we need a new narrative, something that moves us away from dualistic thinking. We need new stories and new ways to see the world.

a new way to see the world.
Diametrics suggest that this over here is good and that over there is bad. It separates rather than brings together. I think it's important to realize that the moment we call something good or a bad, is the moment we reject that love can actually have a say in it. That separation may give us some sense of false peace for a short time, but this way of seeing things has an expiration date. Diametrics ddoesn't allow much space for the tension that light and dark come directly from God or that healing and anger can exist in one person. It doesn't deal with the reality that there are people who are starving in one country and others lost in the illusions of their entitlement in another. We need an entirely new narrative. Maybe the story we have been invited into is one that embraces all of the darkness and all of the light and begins asking 'What can this do with this? How can the light heal the dark? How can peace learn from anger? How can faith learn from doubt? When we begin this process, it allows the opportunity to find purpose in everything rather than creating a black and white world of monotone truths. It drives us to see that all we go through is more than just something that we go through. wonder if its not about the glass, what if the glass was a metaphor for something bigger? Maybe it's a reminder to either

live in the reality that the potential of everything is always possible or to live in the opposite realm where nothing is possible. I think its essential that we come to see that maybe dualism actually creates a diametric worldview where, at the end of the day, there has to be a good or bad[53]. There has to be a dark or light. There has to be a right or wrong. This need to label things might be out of our desire to dominate, to use our charter from God destructively and exclusively. The charter I'm speaking of is the one we were given in the Garden to rule over everything. But dominating and ruling are two completely different things. Even a good ruler allows room for learning, allows space to grow in all areas, a good ruler tends to be quite holistic, or should be. In fact in the Hebrew, the word for tend/rule is *abad* which means to work or serve the land. We might think of the word rule and automatically conclude that we are in control of the earth, yet when we see it from the rich Hebrew language, we see that we have been entrusted to care for the earth. Also, the word keep in the same verse is *shamar* which really means to exercise great care over it. So, God had, from the beginning, entrusted mankind with the huge responsibility of being proactive overseers of what they had been given. My question is, have we? So, when we are told to rule the earth, it doesn't mean consume everything before we run out, it means we are the gardeners of the world. That we all get to work together to keep this place beautiful, lively and inviting. But, we have to be here to do that. If your glass is half-empty and you're ready to abandon this planet, then wouldn't that be denying the discovery of your full potential? Maybe the whole philosophy of whether your glass if half full or not, is more about what reality you choose to live or not live in. Maybe its more about seeing that we are all here for a reason, to live out the reality of God in a prolific, sustainable, grace-giving fashion.

on the need for conflict.

Maybe we can come to a place within us where we can reconcile the reality that God chooses to use conflict to change us. A friend of mine told me this, "God is committed to your development, no matter what!" He was saying this in response to whether I should have left to go from one place to the other. It was so freeing. To know that life isn't about finding some equation to figure out if I go left or right or whether that decision is even wrong or right. We were made to enjoy the life God has invited us into and we should learn to live it well, including the hard times and the good times. To arrive at the same place that Job did about God, which was "you give and take away, blessed be the name of the Lord". Now instead of just quoting a verse and leaving it at that. Let's find out what this means from the Jewish point of view and why its significant to us on the subject of personal conflict. I think it also has something to say about global conflict. Remember the story of Job? He lost it all. Everything. And he was able to come out of this saying what he said. I mean, if I was in that situation I would have probably cursed God. Blessing was an act reserved for rulers. If you lived in a Kingdom or were a servant of a king all you craved was the blessing. Above everything else, you wanted the favour of the king. It was the highest honour. Job says this about God. The word blessed all alludes to a sort of leaping or dancing, a joyful act that was contagious. Job wasn't naïve about his situation, but He was excited about the God he chose. He even goes a step further, Job says that he blesses God's name. In Jewish culture your name was the very essence of your being, it wasn't just a title. It was who you were. Job was essentially choosing the essence of God over the temporal essence of his situation. Not an easy thing to do. But the writers of this story were trying to make sense of suffering and they ended up with the idea that the only thing we can do is let God be God. The end of the book doesn't wrap up the problem of suffering, greed, selfishness, malice, war and pain – it just tells us to dance! Job came to realize that the purpose of life isn't to revel in our misery, again a hard thing to do. But that when the hard times come, when your world falls apart, be reminded that the God who created everything is still sustaining it, and is doing the same for you.

I was adopted at the age of five and was taken away from my family and everything I knew. My reality as I knew it was lost. I had new parents. New brothers and sisters. A new address and phone number to memorize. I had heard about God early on, but we weren't on speaking terms. I didn't even know what it meant to talk to God. I didn't know what it meant to believe, accept or be saved – I was seven. God was this concept out there that was hard to reach and I had to use certain words to try and get his attention, and if I prayed enough He might just respond. But, when I moved into my new home, God and I were silent. The conversation was non-existent. I was told that God did this to me, that he took me away from my parents and put me into a new home. That he was the reason why I was dealing with feelings of rejection and loss. I wasn't very happy with God and I didn't have much to say and it wasn't even that easy talk about the weather with Him. I just didn't feel like I could have the kind of conversation where you can just sit for hours and talk with someone and not even realize a moment had passed. God and I just weren't there. We wouldn't be there for some time. Somehow, Job came to realize something, that sometimes, the things that happen around us are completely out of our control, and that the origin of all that we experience come from God. Job came to a place where nothing else mattered. He used words like 'nude' to give us an emotional picture of how distraught he was. Nudity was shaming in their culture. He had come to a place where he just let it all go. In the letting go, he also found out that it was about choosing who God was over all that he had experienced. Someone's name wasn't just a title like it tends to be in our culture. It was who you were, it was identity and to some even your potential and lasting legacy. It was you encompassed in a word or two.

I have said this before, but, we need to let go. Globally and personally. We need to set down the things that get in the way of dancing with God. Dancing is an intimate state of being where we realize that God leads the steps and we follow. This isn't the kind of dance where we have to figure out the steps that God is leading with physics, its one of trust and reliance. Physics and reliance don't mix well. Physics say we have to figure out how the dance works. Reliance is comfortable with just letting the dance be the dance. The poet William Butler Yeats poses this question "How can we know the dancer from the dance?" Maybe dancing with God is about coming to a place where our steps aren't about whether they are right or wrong, but that we get to just enjoy the steps we take. That we get to enjoy the dancing with the divine. Job knew this. He came to the conclusion that he needed to relinquish his presumptions. Maybe we do to. This is what brought him to say to God that he chooses Him. Who you do choose?

Ghandi once said this "A certain degree of physical harmony and comfort is necessary, but above a certain level it becomes a hindrance instead of a help. Therefore the ideal of creating an unlimited number of wants and satisfying them seems to be a delusion and a snare." Conflicts that emerge are moments of learning. We tend to look at conflict as a personal enemy to our success, but maybe it's the very thing we need to help shape our success. If we run away from conflict we will never change and always be comfortable. That kind of comfort doesn't help us or the world around us. What the world needs are people who know what it means to be alive. And with conflict, we are alive. Without it, we are nothing more than cardboard cut-outs of who we are meant to be. Culture without conflict is a culture that is a pseudo-reality of the real thing. History is filled with story after story of those who rose above some sort of conflict to become part of our pantheon of heroes. The conflict for Rosa Parks was to make a decision on whether or not sitting at the front of the bus was enough to risk her life. She waded through that conflict and has changed the face of Civil Rights. Alexander Graham Bell failed and failed until he discovered how to revolutionize another way for humanity to be in constant connection. And the list goes on and on. But that list is an open one; it doesn't end with these historical heroes. They invite us to follow in their footsteps and learn from them. They invite us to adventure through the conflicts in our life and see them as an inevitable companion on the journey that we could choose to learn from. The more we are proactive in allowing conflict to help shape us, the better the world becomes. The more we learn from it, the more we get to help change the face of history.

Re-examining Corners

He who does not know how to be silent will not know how to speak.
—Ausonius

Silence: To put to rest; to quiet

Silence is the hardest thing for most of us. It forces us into corners we've convinced ourselves that we are not ready to deal with. So we talk. We make noise. We scream. Sometimes the sounds we make hide the pain we feel inside. But, we embrace it. Some of us, call it home. It isn't part of a cycle. It does not follow a natural pattern of progression. It is a way of life. Our televisions fill our already inundated minds with more stuff that we don't need to think about. Getting up, going to work, coming home, eating dinner, having sex, then waking up and doing it all over again. But, in the middle of all that we do, it is up to us to find out what the ever elusive Will of God is for our lives. Some pastors might tell their congregations that there are a series of confirmations that need to happen before you know that is what God wants you to do. Others might say that it comes when we rigorously search the scriptures and find that one verse that seems to direct or guide us. Or maybe all this plus a series of uncontrolled outside events that cohesively work together to help you find your intended destiny. What we must be willing to do, as one of my recent friends said, is to "reexamine everything". God is bigger than our equations. He is more prolific than our Bible verses and seemingly outside "uncontrolled events" that mysteriously lead us to make a decision about whether we go right or left.

the handbook.
When Jesus left his friends with the final charge of "making

disciples", he did not hand them a step-by-step handbook with color photos on how to go about doing it. Why? He trusts them to find it all out on their own. In that, I think He also realized it was going to be different for everyone. So, why is it that when some other follower says something different from what the majority says, they are already wrong before they open their mouth? Remember, Jesus was against the idea that "majority rules". The majority who ruled in the days of Jesus became nothing they were meant to be. It morphed into an institution of people dedicated to preserving all things safe and traditional. Jesus was against that, and if He was against it, why aren't we? Now, I am not saying we should challenge all things that Christendom has given us. There are some good things there. But, we must be willing to re-examine everything. What if Galileo didn't challenge the system? We would still think that the world revolves around us, which honestly, it still seems that way. They called him a heretic and were ready to hang him. So, why is that when someone decides to question things, they to are labeled a heretic? By the very definition, Jesus was a heretic. If that is the case, and we are all his followers, then we too should be ready to be called heretics against the institution, against the empires of religion and oppressive governments. Now, before it seems like I am being combative for the sake of being combative, let me tell you why we are here in this conversation. Because life and God doesn't belong in a box. Too many times we try to keep God, ourselves, and life cooped up in our little boxes that seem to want to make sense of everything. By definition, those things aren't defined by having boxes; their very definitions will not allow that.

the abyss.
There were some 15th century monks who nicknamed God the "abyss". Now, in that culture and time, calling God an endless black hole wouldn't have gotten you the Emmy for the most

popular person. It most likely would have gotten you hanged in front of all of your friends and enemies. These guys were the essential rogue heretics. They were fine with that as a title. Their idea was that God could only be known not by lurking around the edges (which they called theology) but that God could only be experienced by letting go to jumping in. Maybe for far too long we have lived in the Enlightenment age. What if being enlightened is letting go of our enlightenment? Again, it was not about experiencing God through theology. It was also leaving that behind. It was leaving behind frameworks, systems, ideas, and even understanding in place of experiencing the person of God. The person of the Holy Spirit. The person of Jesus. It could only be met in surrender. in the constant context of reexamining everything. I would add that we might need to adopt new words for God, a neo-theology of sorts. We need to make space for the eminence of God; the words we have had are utterly inadequate. I am sure, in years to come we will need more new words for God. Because God is just that big and our words are that small. Formulaic theology and dogma as ways to see God are woefully inadequate as systematic approaches to experience such an experimental God who chooses to redraw the boundaries whenever He pleases. We must be ready to embrace the abyss that is God and remain aware of His ever-shifting dynamic and vibrant soul-altering movement. When we come to a place where we don't feel the need to be in control, then the journey becomes that much more intriguing.

concede.

Way back when people lived in ancient tribes, people sacrificed things. Animals. Food. Children. Adults. The practice of sacrifice was part of everyday life, like shopping is to most of ours. These people believed that if they gave up these things, then the invisible God (someone in their tribe would usually sculpt a wooden image to give them a visual; this says a lot about our need for connection to what we believe in) would in some ways respond by giving rain to dry land or healing a family member from some kind of illness. It was superstitious behavior, but no-one questioned it because it was an everyday aspect of their lives. I wonder if we have similar practices we may not even be aware of that we might need to question. After Adam and Eve decided to take a permanent holiday away from the garden, the first recorded sacrifice we have in the Bible is Cain and Abel. As we know, Cain killed Abel, and we've been trying to reverse that act since it happened. Brothers killing brothers, this story has global implications even now. But why sacrifice? Would God tell the Levites (the personal assistants to the High Priests) that all life is holy and then endorse the pagan practice of sacrifice? This dichotomy is explained in the Kabbalah, a collection of belief and writings within the mystical camp of Judaism. "The Kabbalistic interpretation of the sacrifices are usually associated with the esoteric exposition of the tabernacle and the Temple, whose every detail has symbolic significance in the realm of the *Sefirot*[54] (the ten attributes of God), and with the connection among the individual Jew and the Jewish people as a whole and the divine world, both the good powers and the evil ... it is possible that their detailed treatment of this subject had a polemical purpose - to oppose Maimonides' conception of sacrifice, which denied its intrinsic value and held that the practice originated in pagan customs, which God conceded to the Jews after the exodus from Egypt, because they had not reached a high enough religious level to enable them to worship Him in a spiritual manner[55]"

God conceded to the Jews. God listened to man. I think its important to throw in a reminder here that the authors were writing down their theories and interpretations of who God was in response to their practices. They were creating a hybrid God who conceded to their practices. They were explaining God as one who needed sacrifice to appease his anger. The problem with that assumption is that God isn't angry. If we look at the whole of the sacrificial system as a metaphor and that God conceded to man than maybe what we can learn is that, man has something valuable to say to God, that God wants to hear from us.

equals.

If God can concede to our practices, would He choose to concede to other things of our own design? We see God doing this in the middle of having a conversation with Abraham, the father of Judaism, Christianity and Islam. The conversation between Abraham and his creator happened in his tent. This is not a mistake, God dwells with man. Meeting in someone's tent is one of the most intimate things you could in this culture. It would be like letting someone share a meal with you while holding a knife to your neck. Your life was in their hands. It was a vulnerable thing to do, to let someone inside your home. It was saying "I entrust my life in your hands." I wonder if we have lost this art of hospitality in our culture of fences, guns and iron screen doors. I wonder what it looks like to get it back. Now, it's crucial to remember that around the time that this conversation is happening, Lot has already moved to Sodom. He is among the pagans. He is Abraham's nephew, he is family. In this setting, you didn't define yourself as an individual; you defined yourself by whom you were related to. Your fame or notoriety was deter- mined by whom you came from. This is different from our culture where we spend so much energy exerting our anarchical right to be an individual. Also, you never left family behind. You fought for them no matter the cost. So, enter into the conver- sation between Abraham and God in the tent and you begin to see a pattern. Abraham is bargaining with God here. He thinks he is God's equal. He is so close to God that he believes he can actually negotiate with the all powerful Creator. God doesn't seem offended and He shows no sign of apprehension. He enters into the conversation. He talks with Abraham like an equal. I as well. I wonder if we have lost the art of being close to God. How do we get it back? At the end of this interesting conversation, God concedes. He ends the bargain with His friend Abraham by fully agreeing that He would not destroy the city even if there were ten righteous people. Abraham stepped in for his nephew. For family. God went along with it. This isn't the only story where we see God working alongside humans to preserve life or to increase the opportunity for personal growth. We see this in Moses, Gideon, Elijah and even Jesus. The wonder of God's story is that we get to write with Him.

seasons.

Solomon, the Son of David inherited the ability to write poetry and rule a country like his father did. In one of his most famous works he goes into this list of experiences we all have in life. Although, this list isn't an inclusive list of all things we go through, it is an invitation to see that life happens in seasons. " For everything there is a season, a time for every activity under heaven. A time to be born and a time to die. A time to plant and a time to harvest. A time to kill and a time to heal. A time to tear down and a time to build up. A time to cry and a time to laugh. A time to grieve and a time to dance. A time to scatter stones and a time to gather stones. A time to embrace and a time to turn away. A time to search and a time to quit searching. A time to keep and a time to throw away. A time to tear and a time to mend. A time to be quiet and a time to speak[56]." If you are lucky, you might just experience all these emotions in one day. Life can do that sometimes. You can lose someone dear to you and then you could win the lottery, all in the same day. We are emotional beings. We are made to experience life. Not read it in a book. Go ahead and lay this book down and step outside your door and drink in the moment that is now. Go ahead, it will be here when you get back. Life is about the experience of it. All of it. All the seasons it has to bring. We've been talking about God willfully conceding to man. What if God concedes to the seasons as well?

Now when I say seasons, I mean the seasons of relationship. You can sit in a room with the closest of your friends and chat about anything in the same day; you can both sit in silence and rest in the comfort of each others' company. You can plan a road trip to one of your favorite destinations, or play a game of cards, without ever leaving your living room. You can just be yourself. Although, you have to know who you are before you can be yourself. You can just be. Period. Other than our personal experiences of God, the recorded conversations of God to man are written down in the Old Testament and the New Testament. In fact, one might say that in comparison there is a lot more conversation and interaction between the Creator and the created in the Old Testament than there is in the New Testament. There is much more speaking from God to man. Then Jesus comes on the scene for three years to show what it means to be God on earth. To bring heaven here, now. To oppose systems of oppression and to find peace in the midst of it all. There is so much more we can go into here. As the seasons move on and time rolls forward, God seems to be more and more silent. The other day, one of my friends asked, "Why does it seem that there are more miracles and demonstrations of God's presence in third-world countries than there is here in the West?" One simple answer is that we don't need God enough. We have too much. Our entitlement has become our God. At the heart of that question is the realization that we could be experiencing God a whole lot more. It's as if he was asking, "Where is the God of Abraham, Isaac and Jacob?" The God who kicked this all off. Where did He go? What if God never left at all. He has chosen to concede to the seasons in our relationship. That He has become comfortable enough with us that He has decided to empower us with the ability to heal the world. To reverse evil. To endorse peace. To fight for those who have no voice. God has enabled us with the ability to carry the message of His Kingdom. He believes we can live it out here. He isn't afraid of us getting it wrong. Jesus says to a bunch of his friends that they are the light of the world ... and then a few chapters later He says that He is the light of the world. What He's really saying is we are just like Him. He didn't say one day they will be the light of the world. He told them right then and there that they are the light of the world. His message was overheard by those who might have been deemed as outsiders and dirty by their culture. Jesus was starting to build a sort of revolution. He was saying that all people could be like Him if they want.

The whole idea of Logos that the author John used was that Jesus was this Logos. The Greek idea is that the Logos is the creating, animating force that keeps all of creation together. That Jesus and God are even now still creating. We get invited into that. We get to be a part of the divine artwork we see on display. His dream was to share through the words of Jesus. Ultimately and eventually through us. We are the new Jesus now. We tend to talk about the ominous 'Will of God' as this kind of big, out there in the mist, digging through the mud to see if we might get lucky to find it thing, if there are enough confirmations. This isn't to say God doesn't work this way. What it does mean is that if God's dream has already been given to us through the ancient scriptures then we already have the will of God. Sometimes we think we need to either give more money, take in someone off the street, read more scripture, and maybe do more 'spiritual' stuff. Then the dumb waiter from the sky will slowly, mysteriously appear and life will all be well again. Isn't that reducing life to nothing more than waiting? Were we created for adventure or stagnation? How do we explain to those bloated children who zip across the television screen that we're just waiting on God while we comfortably sip on our caramel frappucinos? I just can't buy into a reality that the will of God is for us to do nothing while others are hurting and dying. This is so much more than what is going in Africa or other countries. A Rabbi was asked why there is so much suffering in the world today and is God going to do anything about it? The Rabbi paused and thought for a moment then responded, "God's answer to suffering in the world is the creation of mankind." Compassion isn't like a new cologne by Mother Teresa, it is who we are. It is who we can become. Compassion is a movement anyone can join in on.Iin Jewish mysticism there is this idea called the *Tzimtzum*, it is the concept that when God created the earth, he held back, he constricted himself to leave space to allow a world to independently exist. God believes we can break the chains of injustice right now, that we don't need to pray how to do it, that by being the answer to our own prayers we are cohabiting the space that God has contracted. If we are to be intentional in our partnership with God then we must learn how to live "after Sinai". "Living 'after Sinai' means that the divine will not swoop, like at the sea of reeds, and destroy the pharaoh-like forces—natural or human-made—that embitter our lives. God may inspire, agitate, and comfort, but humankind must act to create a just and compassionate world, minimizing the pain and suffering of all of God's creations[57]." The dream of God is all over scripture. Fight oppression. Bear one another's burdens. Be peacemakers. Love God. Love one another. Take care of creation. Recapture what it means to follow in the way of the Rabbi Jesus. Forgive without holding on. Bring healing wherever we go. This isn't one of those lists that ends here. There is so much in scripture and outside of it that we can gain from. We cannot chase after perfectionism. It gets in the way of God's grace and redemption. We must chase after healing the brokenhearted. God has put everything we need within us. Being human is a good thing. Jesus came as a human not the divine. Whether he was divine might not be as exigent as much as why Jesus showed up.

If you ever drive on a mountain road that has many twists and turns then you know it is beneficial to have those signs showing you the twists and turns before you get there. The signs lead you to your destination—hopefully in one piece. If you didn't have those signs there might be more metal graveyards lining the bottom of the cliffside. The sign isn't the point. It is what the sign is pointing to that becomes vital. The sign is there to provide us pointers to our destination. To our end goal, or in personal development terms, to our ultimate potential. in scripture Jesus says this about himself: "I always do what the Father tells Me to do…[58]"Essentially what Jesus is doing is pointing his mission back to God. If you read Jesus' words when he begins his campfire parables, they all start with something like this, "The Kingdom of God is like…" He never once says, "The Kingdom of Jesus is like". Why? Because he was the sign to point us to God. God was the centre that he encircled his life around. God was the axis He found his balance in. Sometime people expend themselves over whether Jesus was divine or not. Some might even centre their whole religious experience on this one point. Yet Jesus doesn't point to himself. He is the sign pointing us to God. Maybe we can learn from him. Maybe we are supposed to be sign pointing to God. Whether we think He was divine or not should not deter us from the reality that Jesus didn't come here to die a violent death so we could learn how to appease the gods. He died to show us how love is divine and can truly heal people, places, moments and events through the act of dying to our own rights for the better of mankind. He died to show us that love is much bigger than right or wrong, good and evil, theology and atheism, and male and female to name a few. Yes, we can learn what it means to love through the metaphor of Jesus' death, but there is so much more to it than that. To reduce the death of Jesus to nothing more than paying a debt, would make God the loan shark and us his unfortunate obligated henchman who carry out his dirty work in light of having to appease a global epidemic deficit. The idea that God holds our souls in the balance until we utter some sort of prayer seems a bit too tyrranical and much like a highschool bully who will do anything to get the lunch money she deserves. Which just doesn't seem to fit the God of scripture. Jesus points us to a God who is committed to his creation and not brutally forcing it into some sort of tragic submission. Jesus gives us a picture of who God is in the flesh, and also who we can be with God as well.

To be God in the flesh means we have a responsibility to care for the other. To be God in the flesh means we choose to be responsible rather than imposing our rights. Rights don't leave much room for tolerance. Rights impose, expect and oppress others in the name of inequality. The ancient followers of God didn't believe that we had rights, but that our existence was laced with responsibility for one another. There is an article at My Jewish Learning dot com that says this about rights versus responsibility: "In Judaism there is no explicit concept of rights. There is a system of *mitzvot*, or duties and responsibilities, based on our love for God, where Jewish obedience to law and Jewish fulfillment of obligations are considered a form of divine worship. For example, while the duty to learn and teach is reiterated several times in sacred text (Deuteronomy 6:7, 20-25)—and is understood as an obligation, a tradition, and a cultural underpinning of our essential Jewishness—there is no right to education articulated anywhere." Maybe the only way to make room for understanding is to give up our rights. Our right to freedom, our right to food, our right to clothes, our right to vote, our right to war, our right to say whatever we want. If we choose not to give up those rights than the ability to have those rights should compel us to make sure everyong has those rights too, no matter their worldview or understanding of God. Maybe this is part of what it means to be God in the flesh. To give up our rights like Christ did. To die to our rights to sustain the rights of others. It's a paradox, but one we should uphold because God sees all of his creation as intrisically valuable and significant to one another and to Him.

If we can assume for a moment that Jesus was fully divine and then use that as a metaphor, the implications assume that for each of us to be God in the flesh would signify a need to die to ourselves (as Jesus physically did) to bring resurrection. Being God in the flesh also means to be readily available "to be all things to all people"[59]. Maybe that is what the Apostle Paul really meant, that he came to realize the best him was the one who realized his fully divine potential.

Postcard Images and Bathroom Breaks

"You must live in the present, launch yourself on every wave, find your eternity in each moment. Fools stand on their island opportunities and look toward another land. There is no other land, there is no other life but this." Henry David Thoreau

Our family loved taking road trips. The kind that would take a few days just to plan and get ready for. The ones where all your sister's socks would end up in your suitcase because she ran out of room in hers. We would go from the mythical changing rocks in the painted desert, the arch in St. Louis and to the slums of Tijuana. Our lives were filled with postcard images embedded in our night time dreams, with all the bathroom breaks in-between and the annoying questions of "Are we there yet?" We really got to experience the world as children do. Unedited, raw and beautiful! It was amazing. And when we were young it was so much easier to be fully present.

going to Disneyland.

Children have this incredible knack for being in the moment. When you tell them they are going on a trip to Disneyland, that is all they can think about. No matter what happens around them that moment has frozen in time - their world can even fall apart - but, they are going to Disneyland! When they eventually get there, their world is now the world of Disneyland. Their reality is whatever Mickey Mouse has to offer. Maybe that is why Jesus used them as a metaphor for the Kingdom. The Kingdom seems to be a metaphor for a reality where love is the highest ethic and the invitation is to sustainably live in the moment that never ends. And we live our lives in this moment called the Kingdom in such a way that our lives invites others to live in it all with us. The dichotomy of the child metaphor is that they also have this intense interest in the world around them. Questions abound. It's as if as children, we once had the ability to be lost in wonder. To be in awe of what was around us. They also don't think about things like dualism, original sin, heaven or hell. They just are. They don't get bound up in philosophical debates. If anything, they see everything as connected or non-dualistic. Maybe we can learn from them.

learning from children.
If a parent tells them that they need to get their chores done before they get to go to Disneyland, they don't sit and ponder whether that statement is dualistic or not. They see their actions as being directly related to their 'prize'. It seems a bit simplistic, but dualism wasn't a biblical idea. It was as most things, a human one[60]. It may have been how the world was seen and how most see it now, but the concept started in the neurons of flesh and blood. Seventeenth-century French philosopher Descarte was one of the most prominent thinkers on the subject of duality. The simple version of dualism says that we have a body and a soul. That the world is divided into two realities, light and dark, good and bad, saved and unsaved to name a few of the views that are out there. One of the natural characteristics of living in a dualistic reality is that life is experienced compartmentally and seems to make more sense in tribes and nations. I think tribes though, make us smaller not bigger. More exclusive and more concerned about things like membership, communal approaches to morality, and rigid acceptance of certain dogmas. This is the danger of the dualistic point of view, because if we adhere to it, we agree that life was meant to be lived out in restrictive sections that don't allow for any movement or breathing. If we continue to follow in the way of dualism then there is no room for tension. Without tension there would be no growth or movement. The dualistic worldview makes the "either-or" perspective the hero of the story. It's a worldview that endorses an exclusivist

approach to almost anything it comes into contact with. Are you in? Are you out? Is this right? Is that wrong? Was that light? Should this be dark? The worldview reduces life down to a mechanism. Non-dualism invites us away from the process, into a reality that is bigger than finding answers. As we grow up, physiologically speaking, our bodies go through changes and our muscles experience growth spurts which is done through the natural act of muscle contraction when, at the time, the muscle typically lengthens with the help of tension. Non-dualistic thinking compels us to embrace tension as a friend rather than an enemy. But, I think this way of thinking has to be approached as a child, one who accepts the reality that what they are a part of is more influential than their own existence. If we try to approach this way of thinking through our worldviews that have already been framed by the houses, fences and vehicles that keep us from one another, then the world remains small, minimal, and only full of the possibilities that lie within our own paradigms. It would mean that God can only be engaged from a distance, because we are here and he is there. Some non-dualist philosophers would say that the earth is the mind of God. That we only exist because God has thought of us. If this is true, than each of us rather than a special group of us hold a special place in the mind of God. This leads to the recognition that we are all connected. Connectedness comes with a scandalous realization that we need each other. When one hurts, all hurt. When one smiles, all smile. That our rights don't become the point, but that we get invited into a deeper sense of responsibillity for each created thing. That others would have to come before us. Fulfilling a need is more important than whether you have the right beliefs or not. The greatest belief to uphold is compassion for the other. Not that having right beliefs isn't important, but if we can truly be connected with God then we will discover that God is even willing to suspend his own ego ('beliefs') for the sake of relationship. Maybe that is what the metaphor of Jesus was really about. This reality invites us to let go of the very things that are getting in the way of caring for one another. I don't suppose for a minute, that that is easy. Although it is a much needed shift that needs to occur. Another way to explain this way of thinking is to listen in on some words from the Gospel of Philip: "Light and Darkness, life and death, right and left, are brothers of one another. They are inseparable. Because of this neither are the good - good, nor evil - evil, nor is life - life, nor death death."[61] Maybe this is why it was significant for Jesus to use children as a metaphor. To invite us to "become like one of these" who didn't see the necessity for a disconnected world. To be a people who see that everything we do and don't do affects all of us. When we litter, it effects everyone. When we excessively spend our money and don't use it wisely (or learn to help others with it), then, piece by piece, we begin chipping away the child within. Then the world becomes more about what we gain and less about how we are connected. If we increasingly seek out ways to distance ourselves then mankind becomes distant in and of itself. And that is why it would be dangerous to focus all of our energies on 'getting out of here'. It seems that God needs us to be here. The idea of leaving earth for the mythical city of gold could be easily termed as evacuation theology. Who knows, we might even magically don white robes and grow angelic wings and play harps, however it's going to happen, in traditional theology, we do not stay here for very long. It's as if we're all stuck in an elevator together and we're waiting for the janitor to come to get us out of here. We tend to talk about going to heaven as if we're in a house on fire and we all need to run out of here before it all burns down. We think everyone else are like the inhabitants of Sodom and Gomorrah, that they are unaware of the death and destruction that a loving God might one day bring. And we're Abraham trying to save the few we know that are righteous. What if we have gotten the message wrong? What if we were meant to stick around and rebuild the Kingdom here? The author of Revelation uses the imagery of a city (sometimes called the New Jerusalem) coming down from the skies. God comes to dwell with man. This is what is going on in the Old Testament when we see phrases like a "pillar by night" and a "cloud by day". This is God intimately intertwined with his creation.

tikkun olam.

Steeped in the ancient creeds of these wondering followers of God is this phrase "Tikkun Olam" which when loosely trans-lated means to "Repair the world". To heal or repair the world is a central tenant to the Jewish cosmology. It was the under-standing that we all have an integral part in helping make the world a better place. We each have a role. We have a part to play. In fact, the idea of Tikkun Olam isn't about fixing what's wrong with the world, its realizing that our role here is to scandalously repair the divine wherever and whenever we can. We restore the good rather than focus on the bad. We love the unlovable not because they are unlovable, we love the unlovable because they are lovable. We fight for justice not because justice is weak, but because justice is strong. We find ways to create peace not only because there is war but because peace is intrinsic to the fabric of our world. Paul had this idea in mind when he said, "we are God's co-workers[62]". The actual Greek rendering is even more substantial. It lends itself to the idea that there is synergy between us and God. Synergy is defined as "The idea that the value and performance of two companies combined (entities) will be greater than the sum of the separate individual parts[63]." There is a lot of poetry going on here that we might loose in the English. *Synergoi* is the Greek word here for co-workers or fellow workers It's a term for those who are on equal footing in a partnership of sorts. It's the cooperation of a series of things working together for the end goal. Even in Paul's phrase there is assumption and expectation that God believes we have what it takes. To heal the world. To help repair it. Our culture has taught us otherwise. All you have to do is switch on the television and wait for the commercials to flash across the screen to see that we are subconsciously inundated with image after image of how we are missing the next best thing and that without it we aren't fully us. That we need to find synergy with these pseudo-realities that promise to offer our full potential on a silver platter. Maybe the way to fix this fear of being here is to apologize to ourselves. That we have somehow accepted the lie that we are not enough. That we need more. More of us. The department store Macy's used to run an ad campaign entitled *"More You"* and it was all over the place. You could be walking down the street and see it on the side of a bus, or flip through the different array of channels on your satellite television, or see it on a T-shirt. They wanted to make sure you got the message that they had what you needed to be more you. God made you "you" when you drew your first breath, even before you were a twinkle in your daddy's eye - you were you. And that is what the world needs - you. You here. You now.

The Jews believed that it wasn't our responsibility to fix what was wrong with the world, but that we could all work together to repair the divine in it. It's people coming together and dreaming out loud what the world could be and then working in that divine synergy to see it through no matter what the cost. See, maybe the Church has got it wrong. We spend so much of our time and energy trying to point out what is wrong with the world and forget that God has called it good, and still calls it good. The Hebrew word for good means beautiful. It paints the image of someone who lost all ability for words, someone who has seen something so captivating that their mouth has literally dropped in exclamation. This is God's response to his creation. This is God's response to us. Jewish scholar Abraham Herschel once said, "Maybe its not that man has a God-shaped hole, but that God has a man-shaped hole". God needs us. God has an intense love and fiercely high opinion of humanity. One that has continued since we all drew our first breath. He sees us all as we are meant to be. This is why its incredibly destructive to hurt others, or to allow pain to happen when we can do something about it. We can do something about it.

the end of the story.

I don't know about you, but I am one of those people who like to tell others the end of the story. Yep, I am one of those who like to tell someone the end of the movie even if they haven't seen the movie yet. Sometimes, when I am reading a book I read the end of it first. But, to be honest, I feel like I am cheating on the book, because I am meant to experience it fully. The best thing about going to the movie theatre is that you really don't get to enjoy the experience until after you have seen the movie. But as I am getting older, I am becoming more comfortable with the idea of not knowing the end of the story. I have always enjoyed life as a journey; but that's not a metaphor, life is a journey we get to be a part of. It's beautiful, scandalous, fragmented and utterly inviting. If I spend all my time waiting for 'what's on the otherside', I won't get to experience what is here, What is now. I won't get to taste and see God, because I am wondering what the next dish is. Essentially what is at the core of a lot of theology that I learned growing up was, 'wait till the end of the meal'. 'Get excited about the end of the movie[64].' When in reality, we don't know what happens at the end of the movie. Most people that get to 'see' the end of the movie don't come back and tell us about it. Sure, there might be a few verses in the ancient scriptures that might hint about it, each religion has their own mythology about it[65]. But just because there are stories about it, doesn't mean we spend all of our time thinking about it. There is more to our story. When you know the end before the story ends, you don't get to really enjoy the story now. I would hope we can come to a place where our lives were written to be a part of the story now. Your very purpose in breathing is to be alive. You have been animated to bring life into every situation you get to experience.

waiting.

David was a poet-king of Jerusalem. He was a prominent leader in Jewish history. Revered for his skills as a leader and as a God-follower. He understood hoping and waiting. Waiting was central to his vocabulary. He knew it well. You may know it well too. "I wait for the Lord, my soul waits, and in His word I do hope[66]." The Jewish word here speaks of waiting as an active thing. It's a child who excitedly waits for his father to get home and expends all of his energy running to and from the couch to see out the window when he arrives. It is not a complacently hopeful awaiting for the possible arrival of someone who might come. It is the hyperactive kinetic reaction to the knowledge that God is going to act. Period. That He will respond. It is a word that is interlaced with hopeful action. God has already empowered us with the ability to repair the world around us. There are so many ways we can join in. This is why the language of the 'will of God' that we spoke about before is pervasive if it means we are told to wait in one spot for a big event to happen. Hopeful action isn't waiting; it's doing with the hope of creating space for other things to happen along the way. It is the defiant belief that God is already on the move and that we are moving in and with Him.

The Church seems to have lost its way. It seems to be the lost sheep that Jesus is still looking for. I am not an enemy of the Church; I have great hope for it. I can see its ultimate potential, and I can also see where it has failed, and I have helped get it there. The Church could be more. What does that look like though? If we can see the Church as a heuristic movement, then maybe we can be a group of cultural *mavens* who find ways to engage with the current climate and seek relevant ways to meet people at the point of their need. Heuristics "is an adjective for experience-based techniques that help in problem solving, learning and discovery. A heuristic method is used to rapidly come to a solution that is hoped to be close to the best possible answer, or 'optimal solution[67']".This approaches release the

Church from being an agency of people who are always trying to find ways to force ideas into a certain mold. It means things like ministry become organic rather than trying to create something out of an anticipated need. In fact, if the church adopts itself as a heuristic movement of people than the idea of ministry itself would cease to exist because ministry has turned into something that seems to only survive when a need is either discovered or created.

Maybe churches could be less about teaching and more about living. Churches should be about development in all ways, not about instructing. A movement of people who do not get together to discuss how to be a movement, they just move in their natural environment discovering as they go along how to become a cultural force to be reckoned with. As important as teaching is, maybe a better way to teach could be experiencing what we believe. This is why there is a benefit in transforming and facilitating safe spaces from becoming a building club that meets to engage with people who are willing to embrace a constant shift in formational living. This is what it means to create a heuristic movement. Or maybe the church could be more like a Black Swan event. The Black Swan theory can be explained as "the existence and occurrence of high-impact, hard-to-predict, and rare events that are beyond the realm of normal expectations.[68]" This could include transformational events that have shifted history into an era of positive progression, like the life of Jesus or the life of Mother Teresa. People who have made a positive contribution to the world and have changed the face of history as we know it. Many churches are spending a lot of energy trying to find out how the early followers of Jesus shared community together to somehow duplicate that in their current structure. A problem arises when we try to mimic those in the churches of our past to create the same dynamics of an earlier framework that worked for then but not now. It would be like buying a second-hand pair of shoes that are outdated by 2,000 years and trying to wear them as something new in our day and age. For the early follower of Jesus, maybe what they created for then was their Black Swan event. One thing I think we should come to realize is the questions and approaches we are using aren't relevant enough to speak into the lives of those we encounter. I remember when I was a Youth Pastor in Hawaii and I kept falling on my face. I was still pretty new to the Youth Ministry scene and decided to use all my experience from my college degree to help me build the biggest youth group known to man. Days went by like seasons going through fast forward and nothing happened. Sure, a few people showed up but that was about it. I thought I was a failure. Then one day one of the teenagers came up during a lock-in and told me that they didn't want my programs (another word ministry) they just wanted to get to know me. Maybe the reason why the Church is struggling so much in light of all these cultural shifts is because we have been taught to ask the wrong the questions. Maybe we need a new set of questions. What would it mean to be a black swan event for today? What does that look like? What does it even mean for the Church? Maybe it could mean we are an ever moving, ever progressing movement of people who are committed to seeing the world through the eyes of defiant hope and are willing to find extremely hip ways to engage our society, the broken, the fixed, all of creation with wide open arms and will do anything it takes to change the world. Maybe it also means we have to let go of a lot of our approaches, and maybe even the language and mindset of Church being an approach. Maybe ministries need to go. This isn't about destructively deconstructing everything that the Church has to offer, there are some good things. What it does mean is that now is the time to be transparent about where we are and where we could be. Let's be honest, there is a wide chasm between the two. Maybe a Black Swan event is what we are meant for. Something that changes the course of history. For the most part, it takes a lot out of a church to change the powerpoint background. Something needs to change. And this is a hopeful place to be, especially when we see change as a good thing and not as an enemy.

asaph.

Asaph was this cymbal-playing Levite in charge of David's choir. This rock star used his poetic platform to fight for others. His whole family was so talented they became like the first Von Trapp family around. These poet musicians decided to let their music infuse their beliefs in creativity and progressive behavior. They used what they had to affect change. They were heuristic poets who were committed to being here. Now. And that made all the difference. The danger in never being here on earth is that we don't get to be in on this change. That we don't get to be a part of this act of repairing the divine. Or focusing on the good that the world has to offer. And artistically and energetically, racing after, in numerous opportunities, to help the widow and the poor. The idea of being fully present is an act of holiness according to the Jews. The numerical value of *halom*, (the Hebrew word for here) is the number 75. This is the same numerical value for *Kohen*, the Hebrew word for priest. There is something divine, something deeply holy about being there for someone. The greatest thing the Church could become isn't what happens on Sunday; maybe it's also what happens every other day. Maybe the Church needs to get rid of the Church to find out what the Church is meant to be. The holy act of being a movement of people who are fiercely dedicated to responding to the needs of the world seems to be a better option for the Church. Maybe we are meant to be a body of inclusive people who are more concerned about transforming people rather than theology. It's going to take some guts though, because what it means for those who claim to follow Jesus is the ability to accept anyone into this movement, and for some it might cost you everything. Who knows, this might just be the cross you will have to bear. But, there is life on the other side of that death. All of us will be waiting here for you.

Remolding, Revisiting and Deconstructing

A wise unselfishness is not a surrender of yourself to the wishes of anyone, but only to the best discoverable course of action.
– David Seabury

I get lost quite a bit. I had always prized my knack for being really good at finding things. Since I got married, my bearings have gotten lost somewhere. You see, I am visual learner. I learn by seeing and experiencing. If someone gives me a landmark as part of my directions to get somewhere, I won't get lost. If there are a bunch of lefts and rights without any landmarks, chances are I need my own GPS necklace to carry around. I've got to admit though, sometimes[69] I do that guy thing, you know, where I act like I know where I am going but really I don't. But because I am supposed to be the guy who knows everything and doesn't have the ability to get lost — ever— I project that I have it all together and that I am Google Map personified!

transforming culture.
We were meant to be transformed and to transform culture, people, climates and ourselves. Culture is everywhere. We can't get away from it. To say something doesn't have a culture, would be like saying that the place doesn't really exist. Culture is intrinsic to who we are as people. People, not just places, have culture. You as the reader and I as the writer inhabit a sort of culture. If there were two or more readers than that would be a culture in and of itself. A culture tends to have a certain language within a certain context. Within that context there is also a belief system, an ethical or moral code that tends to be tied in with the belief system, and specific rhythms of life that have either been put there by the forerunners of that cultural group set or new rituals that are currently being created or revisited and revised.

Christianity in and of itself is a culture. The language, ethics, Bible, practices and history all help to define the culture of Christianity. Culture is one of the most powerful influencers of history, and when we understand this we can add to the influence in an effective way. It is imperative that we can come to a place where we realize we too can be cultural mavens and practitioners. Which is really a life long process that comes with an innate responsibility of sensitivity and awareness.

But culture isn't devoid of personal experience and the environment we all grew up in, the places we have come to fear the most and the places we call home. Culture is symbiotically connected to our society and we are connected to it. We can't unculture ourselves. We can deny and slowly move away from cultural practices and beliefs, but our culture is a part of our DNA. Like Thomas Berry the cultural historian once said "The universe is a communion of subjects, not a collection of objects." We can't get away from the fact that our culture is in this communion of subjects. That life isn't objective, it is subjective. it is to be felt and touched and experienced. But, we also have to be honest about our experiences and our limits and understanding. Like my ability to read a map is one such limitation that my ego sometimes tries to overthrow and make me believe otherwise. Either we control the chemicals within us or they control us. This chapter isn't about how bad we are or how limited we might be, it's about how culture helps define who we are and what we believe or how it steers us in a certain direction. This has nothing to do with being a victim of culture, but it does have everything to do with being a culture-bender. Someone who is willing to challenge ideas and ask questions and someone who is willing to choose different colors for the same painting and see what happens. We live and breath and share in this beautiful thing called life. We cannot do that without being honest with who we are as people.

As far as my driving skills are concerned I have since learned that I am even worse when it comes to driving here in England. I am much better at home in California, where I lived most of my life. But our culture says that I should not confess that to you. That my recognition of self-ignorance is the ultimate sign of weakness and therefore informs you that I might have a low self-esteem or need to talk to Dr. Phil. We have to be honest with one another. In fact, our culture says the cool thing to do is hide your flaws, hide your insecurities, and don't let anyone in. It's safer that way. Don't talk about death, don't talk about sex, don't even think about asking the person next to you 'how are you?', they might just hit you. We are afraid. We are terrified to show our scars and share our demons. Yet, there is healing when we do. There is something medically helpful in acknowledging our own baggage. Syd Baumel, a Canadian doctor says this about confession "... baring your soul can not only calm your heart, research suggests, it can lower your blood pressure. Confronting your demons can not only ease your worried mind, it can boost your flagging immune system. Like an apple a day, confession can keep the doctor away."[70]

There is something mystical about letting go of our past junk and then actually meeting the person you were always meant to be.

we need a return.

Teshuva is a word in Judaism that expresses the concept of a return. The Prodigal Son[71] had a Teshuva. He returned home after realizing how destructive his decisions were to himself and everyone around him. He returned home. Life is a journey of returning home again and again. Teshuva intrinsically contradicts our culture of denial and what is 'PC' and what is not 'PC' . Part of coming home involves talking about it, for some it might take place in a room with others where you share your soul in the hope of finding connection and healing and restoration. Then we take all that we have gained and come to understand and do the same with the world. That's what learning is about—so we can apply it. So, that we can "love others as we love ourselves." But we must come to a place of Teshuva before we can move forward.

Madeira initiated three-days of national mourning after torrential rains created a mudslide that has at least killed 42 people along with 120 injured. The world is falling apart. Reality is hanging on a thread. But, I don't need to tell you that. Read a newspaper or watch a news channel and you will see what I mean. The state of the world is not as it should be. We are all responsible for living out what we believe, but in a state of perpetual return. There is a search involved. A community of people needed and willing to go on this search and bring others along with them. Living out what we believe is much more than simply telling others about Jesus. All of humanity is responsible for repairing the divine. This process is going to take time. Returning home always does. If a return is what we need, then what naturally comes with any kind of return is restoration. Healing. Replacing of fear with faith. We must be realistic. We must also be willing to embrace the impossible. That we aren't just Jesus but God on earth as Jesus was. We as his followers must be in a state of perpetual repentance when we choose to follow this Rabbi. Consistently looking at our worldviews and reassessing what we believe and how we are demonstrating that. Also, the word repentance might not be what you think it means.

rethinking everything.

Our family used to go to the beach a lot. We used to spend time on the old rickety wooden piers that seemed to tell stories of those who have walked before. it was beautiful scenery, birds flying through the air like dancers on a stage. One of my favorite things about being on the pier was begging my dad for a few quarters to put in the silver viewfinder that awaited my arrival. It was like a poor man's Disneyland. I stepped up and slowly peered through the two eye-holes and the world was that much bigger and that much smaller all at the same time. It was like looking at the world for the first time again and again.

Jesus could be likened to the silver viewfinder I found so much enjoyment in when I was kid in love with piers. Even before this Rabbi stepped on to the scene, his family was paving the way for his arrival. His cousin John was by this famous river talking to anyone who wanted to hear about this new guy who was going to usher in this other kind of Kingdom. Different to the ones' they were used to. He would use words that they would have known to get them ready for this incoming 'Savior'. John, in the deepest and loudest voice he could muster would shout: "Repent for the Kingdom of God is near!"

Powerful stuff. Repent. Kingdom. God. All these in the same sentence? No one heard of such a thing. It would be like us trying to sit around the dinner table and have a conversation about politics, religion and family issues all in one go. It was unheard of. Before we go further, let's unpack what all these things mean. *Metanoia* is Greek[72] the word for repent. It has nothing to do with sin. When the word is properly placed in its context, it literally means "Think beyond what you know" or maybe even "reform your mind." Somewhere along the way it was adopted by those who wanted it to mean something else other than what was intended. In fact, if you search scriptures there is not one verse that places repent and sin next to each other, unless it directly relates to those who follow God. You may find one or two, but in reality, I think scripture is pointing to something here. If anyone needs to do any repenting, it is those who think they are already part of the club (that was never meant to be). We must be willing to look in the mirror and assess where we are soberly and realize maybe where we are and where we should be haven't met just yet. (But there is hope).

The closest verse we come to is Acts 2:38 which says "Peter answered them, 'All of you must turn to God and change the way you think and act, and each of you must be baptized in the name of Jesus Christ so that your sins will be forgiven. Then you will receive the Holy Spirit as a gift". Peter is saying that they have to become less ignorant and more aware. It's even more than that. He's saying "You have to be more open to the possibility that you may not be living the best life that was meant for you and that you might want to rethink your direction". In first century Palestine, much like today, we use baptism as a symbol or metaphor to signify our "dying of the old man" as I have heard so many times before. Peter is doing that with his words here. He is using baptism as metaphor. When Jesus and John both use the word near in reference to the Kingdom of God, it's the same word we use for "inside". The Kingdom of God is within. It is near. It is around. It is among us.

Maybe the invitation of Jesus to repent isn't solely about what we have done wrong, but maybe it includes a charter to continuously be in the practice of remolding, revisiting, deconstructing and reenvisioning our paradigms. Maybe what we should be repenting of is how we have treated one another or truth or the many other things Christ lists in his sermons. Maybe we should repent for having a hand in the death of those we have tried to "save"[73]. Deconstruction is the ultimate act of repentance. It says we know we need more, and that that more is in the act of understanding what we say we understand. But if deconstruction doesn't lead to reconstruction it's useless. Deconstruction without reconstruction is like leaving a building that has fallen apart to sit in its own decay. And although there are things that might need gangrene to settle in, (e.g., like our over-apparent political allegiance to Western nationalism and empirical arrogance towards other countries) we have to come to realize that we need something more than a taking down. We need a building up. Reconstruction is just as crucial as deconstruction. One depends upon the other. They are in relationship. But to get to reconstruction we have to be alright with where deconstruction might take us. We should also be willing to reconstruct beyond the myths we have created throughout the centuries. Reconstruction doesn't mean we need to find new words to old ideas, it means we need something completely alternative. It might lead us into new territory. It might also force us to ask really hard questions. And we need to ask them. but the moment we stop questioning is the moment our search stops. if the ancient jews were right and truth is unfolding, then the moment we call our findings absolute is the moment that truth has stopped unfolding. this doesn't mean that was has been offered within Christianity hasn't been valuable. what it means is that truth doesn't end with what was canonized (e.g., scripture and etc.) or at any certain amount of councils that were held to create creeds truth became absolute. As vital as they were/are, they are still limited. and asking good questions can lead to even deeper discoveries about who God is and who we are in light of Him. This is why I ask questions, because I want a richer experience of God. and naturally, because the questions by their own admittance 'question' everything, it will lead me into the vastness that is God. which isn't converted to one religion or one 'right' way of thinking. it is seeing that truth is bound up in this endless journey of questions that lead to answers that lead to more questions that hopefully will inspire us to give feet to our ever wandering discoveries. Or as the author Tolkien once said, "not all who wander are lost!74" I think I need to end with the reality that questioning is useless if it doesn't somehow change us, others or the world or all three.

hysteria.

The scene opens in a textile factory where they make dresses somewhere in the US. One by one, the employees began to feel numbness, nausea and dizziness, some experience these symptoms so deeply that they are hospitalized. They all claim to have been bitten by a June Bug. After much research though, no one can find the mysterious June Bug that all 62 employees had claimed to be bitten by. Some later would call this an event of hysterical contagion, where people experience things together within a closed atmosphere and began to believe the same things and taken on the same attributes which tend to be in reality a social or psychological trigger. But because the experience is intense, reality becomes the experience. it becomes the goal rather than the outcome.

In the year 1000 AD, the world was in disarray. Many people believed Jesus was going to return. The belief in Christ's return was so intense that people began believing they were the disciples come back to usher in the ultimate return of Jesus. This was also proved to be a common experience of hysteria.

I wonder if in our attempts at getting to know God we too have been experiencing hysteria? A belief system built upon a mass experience of truth. Where truth is the victim of our hysteria? Where our psychological and socially fragmented views of the world, religion, and religious leaders have somehow painted how we see the world and the things we proclaim to. This isn't everyone (I too fall into this category). I am asking a question of our history, not necessarily now, although the now is an after-effect of our history. I think it is okay if we began asking the hard questions about what we believe and how we have come to believe them.

Let me explain a bit more. Because prominent leaders got together and made some critical decisions about what scriptures we should consider authoritative or not (e.g.,The Apostle Peter was at the First Church Council [Jerusalem]) then, like an act of hysteria, that means we should feel more than inclined to jump onboard? We feel the same things. We claim they all have the same source which is also a symptom indicative of an act of hysteria.

Paul wasn't the only writer of his time. Philo of Alexandria who was a Hellenistic Jew had this view that all the words in scripture were divine, not simply the words that are delineated and separated out by the authors of each work recorded in what we now know as scripture.There were many other contemporaries of his time who were doing considerable things for Christianity as well as other religions. Are we willing to claim that all we have is all that God has said? Are we willing to claim that all of God's authority in spoken word is only contained in 66 books? Couldn't there be more?

Is there more?

If there is more, it doesn't devalue what we have, it just enhances it that much more. Doesn't one of the writers even say that the acts of God/Jesus couldn't be contained in a book? Do we find our origins in a book or in the divine? The danger is if we see God contained in one religious expression, than God unintentionally becomes small. If God is the objective truth, than religions are man made attempts at discovering and naming that truth within a certain context. If one religion thinks it owns God, than maybe it also believes that the earth is still flat. Explorers like Columbus framed their existence on the unproven reality that the Earth was flat and had an edge — until they explored the ocean blue and found that it was, in fact, round. Still, there is a small group of people tucked in the tundra of Alaska who remain thoroughly convinced that the world is flat; they call themselves the Flat Earth Society. They claim that people like Columbus got it wrong, writing in their mission statement:

"Then, in the year of our Lord fourteen-hundred and ninety-two, it all changed. For decades a small band of self-proclaimed 'enlightened' individuals had been spouting their heretical nonsense that the Earth was in fact round. Citing 'proof' based on nothing more than assumptions, half-truths and blind guesses, they dazzled the populace with their 'undeniable mathematical and scientific evidence [...] that the world is shaped not like a pancake, but an orange!'"

I wonder if the spirit of the Flat Earth Society exists in our churches, mosques, temples, and Holy Scriptures? Let me explain. We have evidence — gravity, a curved horizon, and images from space — demonstrating that the probability that the Earth is round is far greater than the probability that it is flat. Most people would agree that the Earth is round. You are not going to see a report on CNN about two countries battling each other over whether the earth is round or flat.

But you might see two countries killing each other on the topic of whether God is on their side or not.

A few months ago, I spent a month in Pakistan doing peace development work. Sometimes, as I engaged in casual conversation with Muslim friends who knew that I followed Jesus, they would comfortably request that I pray to God for them. Not Allah, but God.

Did you see what I just did there? I made a distinction between Allah and God, even if my Muslim friends intended no such distinction. Somewhere in my psyche, I had come to regard God and Allah as if they were individual Greek gods battling for power over the cosmos. This discovery piqued my curiosity to find out what the word *Allah* means in Arabic, and to my amazement, I found that it means "God." Not "the god of Islam" or "the god of the religion who has terrorists fighting in its name," but "God." It's simply the Arabic name for the creator and sustainer of all life. In Christianity we use the word "God" to describe the genderless spirit that presides over not only those who follow him but all of creation. To the Jews the word for the same spirit is *Hashem*; to certain Hindus it's *Vishnu*.

To assume that God resides or expresses himself in just one faith tradition is to assume that God is minute in size, power, and influence. To assume that the creator of the universe can have only one name is like saying that everyone's middle and last name is irrelevant to his or her identity, especially in our society where the last name tends to be especially tied to identity.

Jonah was an Old Testament prophet who lived in the eighth

century B.C. In the story, he believes that God (or Yahweh) is calling him to preach to his enemies, and he isn't a fan of the idea. Assuming that Yahweh is a territorial deity, a god of the land like the other gods he used to follow, Jonah jumps on a ship and flees to the sea, thinking that Yahweh can't possibly go there. As we all know, Jonah becomes a whale's Happy Meal.

After his human sushi experience, Jonah decides to follow through with preaching to the nearby city, and its inhabitants decide to turn from their way of life. But Jonah, unhappy with the way things have gone, decides that he doesn't want to be around for the celebration, so he takes a walk outside the city. Again, Jonah doesn't get it: he thinks this new God is only a god of the seas and some of the land, but not all of it. He doesn't want to talk to this new God. But when Jonah finds a tree outside the city, this new God withers it. It's a reminder that God is everywhere. Some people might need this same reminder.

Joshua was an army captain for the Israelite people whose responsibility was to lead these desert nomads into their new home. In the story of one of the more pivotal battles, Joshua gets a visit from an angel, and like any good army leader, he wants to know whose side God is on. "Neither," the angel responds. The angel then gives Joshua a command to take off his sandals, telling him that he's on holy ground. Even in enemy territory, the Divine is present.

God doesn't take sides. People do.

Wouldn't it be better to say that the Bible is a holy book, a chronicle or narrative of stories of people who have met with the divine? Was this compilation of holy writings meant for us to simply reduce the divine to a few pages or theological standpoints? Or wouldn't it make more sense that it is a book that is alive and that we are drawn to because it resonates with what has been implanted within us...a hunger for the divine? That it is how people have learned to interact with this being they called Yahweh and how we too can interact with Him and learn about Him? And in doing so, we also learn about ourselves. Maybe it was meant to be an interaction of endless discoveries where we too get to join in on the conversation with God.

The danger is that we can too easily arrive (and have so in the past) to a close-ended conclusion that the Book is the point. That our understanding of God can only be discovered in a set of pages. Judaism (where Christianity is birthed from) holds that God couldn't even be named let alone be placed within pages. I am all for a relational being, but I wonder if we have made the divine too human for His own good. Their way of life had origins around campfires where they each shared miraculous intrusions of the divine in their everyday life. There was one shepherd who told a story of how God met him in this bush that was endlessly burning. There was this army general who told a story about how YHWH met him by damping a wet fleece to confirm his Shekinah (Hebrew idea of the presence of God).

The danger is that we can become so distracted by the book, that it actually points us away from the purpose of the book. Which is to invite us to not simply believe in the divine, but to inventivally conspire with the divine and become the change we want to see in the world. To get the world back to what it was meant to be.

But, if we focus all of our energies preserving the sanctity of a compilation of experiences of the divine aren't we actually working against the very thing that those who put it together were trying to do?

When Jesus invites Nicodemus to be born again, it isn't a colonized manual on defining what salvation means. It is an invitation for Nicodemus to lose it all, to give it up, to let go of everything he has known and become like a child again. Then Jesus says something odd. I can almost see it now, like a scene out of the 'The Twilight Zone', the eerie music slowly crescendos and then in an almost ominous manner utters these words under his breath "you must be born of the spirit...to enter the Kingdom of God!" and then the organ plays loudly for effect while Nicodemus' jaw has to be lifted with a crane. Nicodemus scratches his head and asks, "So, I have to go back in my mother's stomach again? That is really weird. It might be uncomfortable." Remember that the Kingdom of God isn't something that is out there in some mist that we have to go groping for. It is a way of life that we are all (and I mean all) invited to join in on. We could join in on the empire. The Kingdom of Caesar. The Kingdom of Obama. The Kingdom of Gordon Brown and etc. But, Jesus is saying that there is a way of life for all humanity (and all of God's creation for that matter), that we are intended to live out but aren't at this moment in history. He has come to demonstrate what that way looks like. It is also crucial to understand that when someone used the word Spirit in the first-century view of the Trinity, it simply meant God. It was a synonym that involved the idea of God moving and breathing among His people. And so this Being invites us back into the Garden of Eden by rediscovering our innocence.

So Jesus tells Nicodemus, a religious leader who would have known the Jewish laws and customs like the back of his hand, that He has to be born of the Spirit. Not a ghost. But of a new kind of culture. A new way of life that is much different to the one he has lived for so long. Nicodemus would have known which spirit Jesus was talking about, but the birth part might have confused him. When the word Spirit was used in the time of Jesus, his audience wouldn't have separated God into three different beings called the Trinity.In the ancient Hebrew world, the Holy Spirit wasn't viewed a third entity of what we call the Trinity. The word spirit was a synonym for God. Let's unpack this conversation a bit more.

Menahhemana, is the Syriac word for spirit. It means life-giver or one who resurrects others. In essence, Jesus is telling Nic that if he is really interested in joining in on the Jesus experience then what he has to do is first realize that the life he is living isn't giving him life. That the life he thinks he is part of is more like the Matrix. Nicodemus is one of those that are linked up and needs to be disconnected. I think we all could do with a bit of disconnection. And if he chooses to let it all go, to realize that there might be a better way, then he can give in to this life-giver. This spirit. This new way of doing things. The one who brings things back into life. Again, it can't stop there. Once we choose to join in on this new way of life, then we find ways to compassionately live it out within our personal contexts. We partner with other cultures, religions and circumstances and seek out ways we too can bring resurrection and life into hopeless situations. The resurrection of hope to one who has lost it all. The resurrection of peace to those who have none. The resurrection of grace to those who may have forgotten what it means to be loved.

In the Greek world, baptism was used for objects as well as people. They would dip objects into the water to commission their use as we see in the Greek adventure story written by Xenophon entitled Anabasis, "These oaths they sealed by sacrificing a bull, a boar, and a ram over a shield, the Greeks dipping a sword in the blood and the barbarians a lance." The word they use here is the root word for baptism. It refers to the idea of preparation for something great like a wedding or a celebratory procession. It is also invites people into something bigger than themselves. It was a picking up and a laying down, the essential ying and yang spoken of in Buddhism or the harmony of the opposites that Solomon talks about in the book of Ecclesiastes.

I wonder what we have that we need to let go of and recommission to be part of a bigger story. What theologies do you have to let go of to meet God where He is? Nicodemus had to let go of a quite a few. Maybe you and I do as well. To join in on this way of life that seeks to change you and then challenges you to go and change the world around you. You see the message of Jesus isn't that we simply learn and keep what we know, but share it by living it out on a daily basis. And here's the beauty of it all, we don't have to get it right the first time.

Safety First

Avoiding danger is no safer in the long run than outright exposure.
The fearful are caught as often as the bold.
– Helen Keller

I have a Facebook and a Myspace and I belong to four other random online communities. I am on the Facebook Oregon Trail and Mafia Wars. Facebook makes you a celebrity in your own world. You are in control of what others can know about you. They allow you to create a person that you may not be, along with a past that may never have existed. In a word, sites like Facebook give you — safety! Don't get me wrong, it can be addicting and can also allow for some really beneficial networking opportunities. It's relationship education with training wheels. We learn who to be, who we want to be and how to be. But maybe there is even more to Facebook than our status updates.

There could be more to these online communities other than Linus's blanket? Remember him, he was Charlie Browns' friend in the Peanuts gang comic. I used to wake up every Saturday and Sunday just to read the comics. Sure, there was more to life than this, but come on, we're talking about comics here. Linus never let go of his blanket. In fact, he held on to it so long that occasionally you would see him hiding behind an ominous smoke cloud like Pigpen.

Are we like Linus? Do we hold onto to our online worlds so fiercely that they are cloud that we hide behind?

Maybe we hold onto them because in some weird sense they hold onto us. Take a week off from your Facebook and listen to your internal dialogue and write down what you hear. And see how Facebook might have changed how you relate to others. Maybe we are afraid that if we let go of our online persona's than

Jesus Bootlegged

the dust might clear and people might really see us for who we are. We've been taught that that might be a bad thing. Who knows, we might even have to deal with who we think we are. Escaping is central to an online community, in fact, some might even say that is the only reason they join them — to escape. Some people only read fiction books. They love to dive into other worlds, to escape the one they live. They want to believe, for a period of time, that the world they call home doesn't exist. They want to be a part of this newfound world with endless possibil- ities. in fact, fiction books are the widest read books out there. This informs us that maybe fiction has become truth and has become our new kind of blanket that we hide under. We now live in two worlds, the one where people breath in and out, and one where wires and megabytes and fictional narratives tell us who we are. You see these places keep us from being rejected. They let us be who we really are without apology, in the real world, that is not such an easy thing. A world drenched in unspeakable dangers and "what if's"; so escapism is the new safety. Places like Myspace allow us to join a community without the commitment. Community is way too messy, way to unsafe, way to risky for most of us to take our masks off. So for most of us, pseudo- community will have to do. Maybe in the corners of your bedroom as your typing away, creating another online person- ality, you hear voices that tell you are not good enough, you do not have what it takes. Maybe those voices are familiar ones, maybe way too close to home. Your mother, father, brother, or someone who has value in your life. Others might have made a random comment that you have held on to you for years. Half of the talk shows that are still on television, invite guests to share personal stories about what happened on their school playground, when someone called them fat or ugly or weird and how those words stuck with them and drove them to lose weight or get a new nose, but the sting of those words still resound. Shows like this show that the topic is still a large part of our culture. Somehow your belief in those destructive words has made them truer than they really are. God is having a conversation with Abraham and tells him to leave everything. This dialogue between the divine and the created starts in Genesis 12: 1 – "Now [in Haran] the Lord said to Abram, Go for yourself [for your own advantage] away from your country, from your relatives and your father's house, to the land that I will show you[75]." Rabbi Zushia, a Hasidic Jew shares some insight on why God may have started Abraham's adventurous charter with 'Go to yourself...'"When I get to the next world, the World of Truth, if they say to me: 'Zushia, why weren't you like the Baal Shem Tov[76]?' That's not going to frighten me one bit. How can you compare me to the Baal Shem Tov? And if they say to me: 'Zushia, why weren't you like the Maggid of Mezrich[77]?' That's not going to frighten me either. Look at me and look at the Maggid of Mezrich! What frightens me is when they say to me: 'Zushia! Why weren't you Zushia! The Zushia that you could have been, why weren't you even that?'" "Go for yourself" can also be translated as "Go to yourself...." The mystical sources explain this to mean: "Go to the root of your neshama (soul)." In the next world, there will be no claims against a person that he failed to live up to the potential of others. However, it is our duty to maximize our talents, to push out to the very limits of our abilities so that we bring the root of our souls to flower. It is only in this way that we will be, at least, our own "Sushi's." We must come to a place where the things outside of us don't define us. If we commit ourselves to the journey of discovering who the Divine intended us to be then the world already becomes a better place. Instead of answers, life becomes more about the discovery.

life as a bus.

You meet all kinds of different people on the bus. One day, you might meet the ex-president of a large nearby company. Another day you could meet a woman who is barely making enough money to pay for the bills or put food on the table. You might even meet someone who is a high-powered broker who's car broke down and he's trying to make it to a meeting that will make or break him or even a pastor on his way to a wedding that he's officiating. The bus is a place where all people become one. A community on wheels. A mobile movement of diversity. I wonder if we can use the term church when we talk about things like this. The word for church used in scripture was a gathering, but not just of religious people but of anyone. It was a word typically used again as political jargon to describe a group of people who supported their leader of choice. Church was about who and what you supported and how you were going about trying to live out those principles wherever you were. Any kind of community can be called a church or gathering. And that means we could learn from one another. Share life with one another. Break bread with another. And even love one another. Church isn't an event, it's a community of people anywhere and everywhere learning what it looks like to enjoy life as we know it and use that joy and find ways to bring it into hopeless situations. Community is also about diversity. I read somewhere recently that "divinity is in the differences[78]", the things that make community what they are, tend to be the diverse things that bring them together. Homogeneity could be the death of the Church if it continues. Homogeneity doesn't breed diversity. Maybe we need to redefine what the Church should be. Maybe the ancient church had nothing to do with what we are now. I have heard many people who desire to be just like the first-century church and want to copy their models and approaches, but the danger than is we become more like them and less like us in the here and now. There are some good things we can learn from them. But who they were then was for then, and who we are now might not be good enough for what they might need then. So, maybe we need to dissolve certain aspects of the church. Maybe we need to get to a place where we can sit and dialogue about change and invite everyone to join the conversation. Everyone. Maybe we need to tear down barriers that seem godly but really aren't. For some, this might mean selling the building and starting all over. For others it might include a total makeover, theologically, mentally and physically. But to be sure, the Church as is, is inadequate. It's not what it was meant to be. And we need to recapture her as a movement of people that transform societies through love.

Again, this does not mean that we should throw away all the things we believe, but it does mean we should not be scared to ask questions or to seek answers that might even lead us out of the boundaries we have made for ourselves. We have to remember that most of our theology has been framed by our environment, history, upbringing and worldviews. Even our understanding of God has been moulded by these very things. Origen, who was one of the most prominent God scholars of his day didn't one day get a vision from God with all the answers to life. If he did, I am sure he would have remembered to write that one down. We have to understand that our comprehension of the divine is already limited, not because of our sin or even because we are finite, but because God on his own is too vast for one being to discover all of Him. The reality is, if we have been following a god comprised of our understanding, than we've been following the wrong god. And if we've been following the wrong god, then there must be a death. Not ours — his. Nietzsche blamed the Church for killing God, unfortunately, I think we have to do the same. It's useless for me to sit and point the finger when I myself am part of that system. I think we might need to dive into the world of design to find one possible solution. The word design tends to be riddled with ambivalence when used in the world of design. It allows a lot space to play and to discover. We can't get away from the reality that we are subjective beings trying to understand God who is outside of our subjectivity and who is also a part of it. Our beliefs by nature have some sort of influence from our subjective way of being and seeing the world.

But it is the differences that creates other differences, and those differences breed even more differences. And differences aren't right or wrong, they just are. Differences invite discussion rather than repel it. Diversity invites us to see that truth, God, love and other ideologies were and are bigger than Christianity. They are more convincing than simply being a system of beliefs. They are things that helped order the cosmos. These ideas are part of a microcosm we all call home. Diversity invites change. Change invites growth. Growth invites movement. Movement invites transformation. And when this experience of community happens, the divine is present in and among those together. We are most like the divine when we are in community.

microsoft god.

One of the most overused phrases in scripture is "In the beginning God created the heavens and the earth[79]...", it also one of the most easily overlooked phrases in scripture. You may have heard that the Hebrew word for God is *Elohim,* it is a word that describes a pluralized form in one name. It would be like saying, "Microsoft offers some of the best computer products out there". Even though you use the word Microsoft, you are referring to the people who work within it. According to Christian thought, God is Himself, Jesus and the Holy Spirit. The three make one.[80] God is in community. He works in community. He himself is community. He also invites us into that community. There is painting that shows an old tattered iconic image of three angelic-like beings sitting at the same table together leaning in. Let's dissect this a bit. Leaning in was a posture of intimacy in the first-century. In the middle of the table is a bowl, a metaphor for communion or oneness. Yet, the peculiarity of the photo is that there is an opening at the front bottom center of this Russian icon; the implication is that we are invited to join. Maybe the invitation extends to anyone who sees this picture. Anyone. God is not afraid to invite all of creation to be equals. To share in his divinity. To be a community. Not just the Church. All of humanity.

the shema.

The Shema Prayer [81] is an ancient prayer that happens to still be in use today by many practising Jews. The Shema: "...is the first prayer a Jewish child learns. The word "Shema" means Hear and that is the first word of the prayer. The prayer was developed as a summary of the whole of the Jewish law. The prayer is taught to all Jewish children by the parents and thus emphasizes the responsibility of parents in passing on the principles to their children. The Shema is the central focus of Jewish worship." This prayer is integral to the spiritual development of any Jewish child. Part of the words of the prayer are as follow: "Hear, israel, the Lord is our God, the Lord is One" The word for one is Echad. it denotes a picture of unity. Of working together. in some Jewish circles, it is also interpreted as unique, different. in this one verse we see God laying out how man should be, how all creation should be working together as he Himself does - in community. israel is a nation, a group of people. A community. God tells Abraham that He intends to use him by making him a pretty influential guy, he uses a Jewish title and calls Abraham "...a father of many nations[82]" This would have been the first ever episode of the MTV show - MADE (where people who have never had a chance to become what they have dreamed are given the opportunity to chase it). Abraham is the "father of many nations". He is going to start something global. But see it doesn't stop with him being chosen, the chosenness isn't the point. It's what we do with it that determines what happens with what we have been given. I think too often we keep what we have, because it is comfortable. Our habits form this blanket that keep us warm. Warmth makes us feel safe. And our safety puts the world in danger. We can no longer afford the safety of our pews and chairs and our own versions of truth to lead us along. We must become an active community that intentionally and incarnationally looks outward. Now this next part of the Shema is what takes us into all kinds of interesting directions. But it should at the end lead us to one. As I was saying earlier, the word for one means either unity or uniqueness. Maybe this word was chosen not just so we would know who God is but also how he works and how he invites us to work together like him. It means that in our uniqueness and differences we all come together and work to rebuild the world around us. Christians. Muslims. Atheists. Buddhists. homosexuals. The list goes on. To recapture hope where it might have been lost. To find peace where it may have been covered in the rubble of war and things left unsaid. To instill grace in situations where there seems to be none. To be God where He seems to not be present. To be the answer to our own prayers.

I was at a BBQ on a roof in Pakistan, eating the backside of a chicken with a pastor. We were talking about different approaches to church and different ideas about God. That time with the pastor got me thinking about my time there and how in a place like Pakistan everything is a communal activity. Everything is experienced community. Family issues aren't resolved by asserting one's individuality. They are met head-on as a family. In community. If you lose someone dear, going into your room for alone time isn't an option. Mourning is experienced as a community. As Westerners, it seems we have lost the art of being in community. We have the media, our culture and our childhoods that are puppets of individuality that inform us how to be and what to believe. But it doesn't stop there. Even the elusive American dream tells the story of how one man or one woman comes over to America and gets the house, and gets the car and the beautiful wife and finds eternal happiness. The story never involves a group of people experiencing the dream. It never seems to allow for the reality that this might happen for a community. In this country, it is about the individual. Somewhere down the road we have forgotten that the individual is meta-epistemic which means, we are a part of the whole. We alone don't make up the whole. And so maybe the first step towards the whole would be trying to work together not separate. It's relearning what it means to be tribal without the exclusive nuances oozing out of the cracks. We need a new approach to communal life. It's about sharing and learning that what is mine isn't mine, it's 'ours'. This won't be an easy road to walk, because you might find those who like being the lone rangers, those who would prefer to go it alone. But, this is why hope is much more than a cliché. Hope is tenacious and greedy for more hope. So, we have a choice, let the circumstantial rejection of our ultimate potential colour everything or we take the hand of hope and enjoy the ride. Because, we can't afford to do this alone. There is nothing wrong with being an individual, but somewhere along the way we have come to believe that our individuality is the point. We have songs and television shows that praise the life of the "lone wolf" or the "loner". Yet, in just two years of being here, i have discovered something about the peculiar people of the mythical ageless lands of the UK. Even though there are glimmers of the individuality that we so highly commend in the States, there is an overall sense of community within the walls of this country. There are programs specifically designed to help those in need. There are organizations that are in place to keep people from becoming homeless. There are so many other examples that could be shared here, but the point is this, there is community here. We could learn a thing or two from our history in regards to community.

a history of community.
Way before the ages of the Renaissance and Enlightenment, humans lived in community. We breathed our first breaths in community. We call them tribes. They called it their way of life. The Paleolithic period of hunter-gathers, lived and shared life in

community. They started their lives in community and they ended their lives there too. According to sources[83], "...Human societies from the Paleolithic to the early Neolithic farming tribes lived without states and organized governments...Middle Paleolithic societies, unlike Lower Paleolithic and early Neolithic ones, consisted of bands that ranged from 20 to 30 or 25 to 100 members and were usually nomadic. These bands were formed by several families. Bands sometimes joined together into larger "macrobands" for activities such as acquiring mates and celebrations or where resources were abundant. By the end of the Paleolithic era about 10,000 people began to settle down into permanent locations, and began to rely on agriculture for sustenance in many locations. Much evidence exists that humans took part in lonGodistance trade between bands for rare commodities (such as ochre, which was often used for religious purposes such as ritual and raw materials, as early as 120,000 years ago in Middle Paleolithic." Man lived in community. They even searched for resources together for their communal religious experiences. They were not scared of the possibility that what they believed might have more commonalities than not. For centuries theology has been this sort of belief system bound to certain set of principles or strict guidelines called doctrine and dogma. When they started out, it seems that faith tenants were never the point; they were a loose guideline to lead us into new discoveries. But over time, like shoes, they can all get muddied and what was can no longer be seen or noticed. and they can get worn out and get holes in them and the only thing to do is to buy new shoes. Maybe we can see words about God as this art form we all get to paint with, and maybe even something that those outside of our initial faith group get to help us with. To help decorate and discover the potency of God whatever that might entails. So if we adopt theology as an art, there is a lot more room for discovery, a lot more room for possibility. Maybe even a lot more room for God to breath. seeing theology as something to develop rather than something that is already developed allows God to inabit the spaces we have yet to find. It allows for anyone, laymen and the inexperienced especially, to enter and add to the conversation. Maybe we can also adopt another metaphor as well. if we can think of theology as a poem...then we each can add a line or two to the stanza's and add to the vastness of God. We can begin seeing that God can surprise us like a sunburst on a rainy day. or a smile from the most of unexpected strangers. We must be willing to be surprised if we are going to make the shift from doctrine to art.

theological surrealism.

The surrealists were rebels in the art movement. They worked under the premise that life was this huge surprise we get to experience and uncover. They put things together that might not naturally fit.They were lateral thinkers.They lived and breathed in the world of irony. They embraced the tension between light and dark. Rather than attempting to define their world by calling it dualistic. The artists were intentional about starting a revolution. They belonged to this particular group that was nicknamed DADA, they emphasized and embraced unpre-dictability as a way of life. This is the same for those who embrace theological surrealism. Theological surrealists paint with a different brush. They believe in an anarchic hope, a hope beyond what is a hope of what could be. This new kind of hope sees the world caring for its resources and being 'green' not because it's the latest fad but because we have a responsibility to care for the earth and the resources. As it has been said, the more we take the less we become. This new surrealism believes that theology isn't just the study of who God is, but it is the living out of those discoveries. It is the application. It is a rebellious idealism against systems that would seek to label it or try to control it as a movement. Like singer John Lennon once said "Surrealism had a great effect on me because then I realised that the imagery in my mind wasn't insanity. Surrealism to me is reality." Its painting the world with a different brush. We sometimes use the word surreal to mean that a situation or experience is beyond reality. What Lennon might say is that the 'beyond reality' is the new reality. Without being too pseudo-modernistic here, I believe in reality. But, I believe that all of reality also encompasses some of what we say reality is not. So maybe what we can do is come together and start the process of deconstructing what we have come to call Christian reality and reconstruct a more suitable place where all of humanity can live. I think there is a difference between the reality that Christ spoke of and the reality that Christendom espouses itself to. One says everyone else outside of it has to join us, the other former offer an invitation for those who want to join in on this way of life to partake in it even more intentionally. There maybe people who don't necessarily use the label Christian but are still contributing to this new global reality. Surrealists realize that they are offering a picture of the world, not the picture of the world. That arrogance takes a back seat to formative invention and in its place is the gift of humble offering. That's what it means to be a theological surrealist. Someone who is willing to share how they see the world but only as dialogue and nothing else. For centuries we have been taught that to follow Christ means to force others to see the world the way we do, and now we're just starting to realize that that is not how Christ operated. If anything, He came to liberate us not to imprison us into a new way of life. This newly discovered epiphany about Christ, coming to offer rather than force, is very counter-cultural to our society, assumptions, biblical interpretations and church services. Theological surre-alism is much different to theological education which tends to be used as a way to arrogantly assume that knowledge or bible verses are going to fix relationships, poverty, injustice, debt and the world crises so prevalent in our morning newspapers. This doesn't mean that the Bible has nothing to say to today's' crises, it just means we have to actually start living it all out. But it seems that a lot of people are concerned with the tension of living in the world and not being of it. Yet, we are made to be here now. I think that tension isn't our enemy. In fact, I think we read it all wrong. We have to live in this world if we choose to be alive. The not being of it might just allude to the reality that life is transitory. It doesn't mean that we are supposed to, on some level, be at odds with the world or its culture. I think it's a metaphor for how life is fleeting. It's as if Christ was praying that they would live life well while they are alive. That they would find ways to be the Kingdom in the there and then. Its a challenge for all of us to be the Kingdom in the here and now. It's like someone saying there is more to life than life itself. I believe this is what is going on here when Jesus prays these words. You see, theological surrealists are more concerned about creatively thinking of ways to setting the world right. And upsetting the status quo and living on the edge of stereotypical ways to see the world. They perpetuate intentional acts of grace and they are less concerned whether someone is a Calvinist or Armenian. They believe that the world is worth living in and that love is the highest reality or canvas that they can paint on. At the centre of theological surrealism is the idea that tension is a good thing, something we can come together and dance with, discover, and create new ways to see the world and bring that into reality. Tension as God as divine and yet vulnerable. God as creator and the created. God as dark and light. Despair and hope sitting in the same room. Peace and turmoil sharing a mailbox. This new worldview gives us the goggles to see everything around us with a new way to believe and create. It is a more adventurous way to see things. Theological surrealism allows space to accept the uncomfortable reality that Jesus is bigger than Christianity. That the message of Jesus was not for a few, it was for many. For all of creation.

In the movie *Instinct*, Anthony Hopkins plays Dr. Powell, an anthropologist who ventures out into the African jungles to spend time with and study the life and community of gorillas. During his time with the animals he discovers a common brotherhood with them, but even more so that we don't know how to give up our dominion. That things like having freedom or control are Illusions we think we have. The first step to becoming emancipated is to accept that we live in a world of illusions. That isn't to say the space we inhabit is a mirage or that we are not flesh and bone, it is to invite us to see that the life we live becomes less about what we know or how to control it and more about experiencing what the journey has to teach us.

The enemy of community is control. Fear. The more fear the smaller people get. The smaller a group of people become no matter how large the numbers. God essentially says to Abraham, "I want to make you influential. For the world". We are all meant to be greater than we really are. The assumption in the ancient Jewish life is that it can only be done in community. God is a community. He chooses a group of people, a community. Then He sends that community out. Community. Community. Community. I don't presume that living in community is easy. There have been times when I have wanted to walk out the door, and have. Community is messy. But once we think we don't need the experience of community then our worldview and our fear of tension take the driver's seat. How you define that community is up to you. What it looks like when you actually are part of it is completely different for each person.

The night before Jesus was heading to the cross he prayed. But he did not want to do it alone. He got some of his friends and told them to sit at a nearby tree and he even asked them to pray for him. In Matthew 26, Jesus tells some of his closest friends to "Watch and pray, that you may not enter into temptation..." Jesus asked for prayer? Yep. He was going to go through one of the most horrific deaths of all time and He didn't want to be alone. He wanted friends around. Have you ever had one of those moments? One where it seems like your world is going to end, and there is nothing you can do about it except share your agony with those around you? This is what it was like for the Son of God. Then He goes into one of the most interesting prayers recorded by John, it was recorded as if John was there in person hanging on every word. The assumption is that he disciple didn't fall asleep. Out of all the things Jesus could have prayed, He chose to pray for us. For the world. Not for world peace. Not for Himself or that He wouldn't feel a thing hanging on the tree. But, he prayed that we would all be one. One. There's that word is again. Jesus is purposefully playing on the Hebrew word "echad" here. Jesus sees this idea of being one not as some idea to be marketed in the ever-growing place of post-modernism or any other place for that matter. He sees this oneness as a way of life. A way to live life. This doesn't mean that you have to close this book and go live in a commune; it means you learn how to embrace community where you are right now. Jesus prays the prayer in such a way that He believes we can actually be one. I also think it was a larger metaphor for how the world could work together, a blueprint for humanity. It would seem, if that interpretation is correct that Jesus believed that we could all be one. This is deep stuff. Jesus believes something, that it seems, our actions throughout history and even now say we believe otherwise. His beliefs about mankind come out time and again. Not only mankind but even his closest friends. He says this in His prayer: " I will be in them, and you will be in me. So they will be completely one. Then the world will know that you sent me. And the world will know that you loved these people the same as you loved me.[84]" Jesus is inviting us into something compelling here. He is saying that when we are all in community we are most like the divine. Like God. We are just like them. And then He even goes on to say that when we are in community that somehow that oneness will be so loud that the world will want to be a part of it. This is powerful stuff. Jesus believes that community has the power and influence to help change the world. Being in community is an act not a belief.It is something that happens and occurs and keeps occurring. He even takes it a step further, Jesus says that the act of being a community is good enough to actually have others meet God in an intimate collision course. The word "know" in Hebrew is one of intimacy. Jesus isn't talking about "salvation" as we know it. He is talking about experience. Community happens when we realize that we can't do it alone. That we weren't meant to do it alone. That when we come together and are one, than we can race toward the same goal and be there for one another. In that act alone, it somehow is more than enough to change the world.

Flowers, Birds and Humanity

No culture can live if it attempts to be exclusive.
– Ghandi

Jesus took on the culture of humanity in all its fullness; or as William Young says in the Shack, " It would be like this bird, whose nature it is to fly, choosing only to walk and remain grounded. He doesn't stop being the bird, but it does alter his experience of life significantly." Jesus never stopped being God, but He did choose to use those rights sparingly his whole time on earth. Later, Jesus says, "I only do what the Father tells me to do" verifying that He willingly chose not to fly. Humanity is not the enemy. How we choose to use our humanity can be the enemy to our progress as created ones. The conspiracy of Jesus doesn't see culture as the enemy but as the trail leader that leads us to discover innovative outlets to empower others to join in on the redemptive plan of God. Having said that, I think that there are things in our culture that we have embraced but that we should have abandoned long ago. Things like consumerism have crept in the backdoor of our churches and have reframed the way we read scripture[85]. For example, when we read the conversation between God and Abraham - God told Abraham that He was going to make him a "... father of many nations" - we think the phrase signifies that Abraham has to find ways to get as many people into the fold as possible. When the words themselves in context mean that he will influentially leave an indelible mark on creation through his lineage and life. Numbers do not determine success. Numbers create the illusion that we are doing the right thing. Hitler was successful in getting quite a few people supporting his cause, but that doesn't mean he was doing the right thing. Or David Koresh, the cult leader from Waco, Texas, who got a lot of people to believe and follow him into their deaths. Converts don't determine how well we are doing. Our lives do. Our integrity. Our words. How we treat each other. And how we don't. These are ways in which we might determine how well we are doing. Things like love ,goodness, truth, faith ,hatred, greed, lust, perfection, salvation, grace, and peace — these aren't Christian or religious in nature. They are virtues that naturally exist beyond this reality and invite us to follow after them. They did not one day make a decision to convert themselves to follow after Jesus, Buddha, Mohammed, or any other religious leader. They are what they are. The fact that we can't let me be themselves means we are not comfortable with ourselves. We tend to try and change/convert things so we can either relate to them or make them more comfortable to handle.

The word success with the current connotations should be stripped from our vocabulary. Like a line from the movie Elizabethtown that concludes "In that moment I knew that success, not greatness was the only god the entire world served." The current ideas of success have been a bedfellow with consumerism for far too long, it is time for a divorce that should have happened many years ago. Consumerism says 'we need more, more, and more'. Success says that 'I will do whatever it takes to get that more'. When we read the Bible, I think we have to come to accept the possibility that the way we read what is before us is tainted by consumerism. What if God meant something entirely different when He told the Israelites to "...go and take the land I have given you..."[86]? As a Westerner we might hear these words of out context[87] and apply the laws of consumerism and think God is talking about actual land somewhere. But when you read it from the Hebrew it might say something different. At the beginning of that verse God has sent Israel out to this particular place called Kadesh Barnea which loosely translates as "holy wandering". The word for sent in Hebrew is *shalach*, it is a charter that has been given to these wandering people to go and discover, to see that their wandering isn't purposeless. Later, God tells Israel that He has given them the land. The word for *given* connotes a sort of gift. But a gift with a responsibility. Like when someone lends you their most valuable 'thing' and expects you to take care of it. The word for land is *erets* in Hebrew, it can either mean land or earth. So when we relook at this verse word-for-word, maybe it never had anything to do with consumerism, but maybe it was a metaphor for something bigger, something momentous and even more scandalous. Maybe God is reminding the Israelites that He has entrusted them with the responsibility of finding him on their holy wanderings. That the earth is their playground - in malls, in stores, in movies, in mosques, on Sundays and on every other day of the week. It's a reminder to us that He is even in music, in movies, in pain, in laughter, in sin, in separation, in brokenness and in many other things and places. God wants us to see that He is bigger than all of us yet can also be seen in one another. God gave them (and us) the gift of insatiable hunger to go and find him everywhere. That they are to infect people and invite them into a scandalous journey of endless wonders. It might be too easy to see these words laced with consumer ideals and success-driven bifocals and think God would be telling His people to go and the annihilate sacred life that the Jews held so dear. If we follow consumerism down to where it lives, all we can bring back with us is the hell it evokes. Really at the heart of consumerism is the heartbeat of 'keeping up with the Joneses' and that little credo has gotten countries like America into a lot of unnecessary trouble. What is 'keeping up with the Joneses' really about? Its this hunger for acceptance, validation and self-empowerment. So, really consumerism is about us and how it makes us look and feel good about ourselves in comparison to those around us. If that's true, than that philosophy of trying to keep up will either consume our lives or consume the earth, whichever comes first. The process of consumerism leads to entitlement, which then leads to oppression. We have a history of examples that have followed this cycle. Rome. Israel. America. To name a few. If we think something is ours, we will do whatever it takes to keep it. Whatever it takes. Consumerism has killed the church. So, we need something completely different. What if we started seeing each other as influencers - people who influence their world? If we follow this way of thinking, than the act of being an influencer would lead to giving. Because embedded in the act of influencing is the desire to give that influence away to help transform others. If our desire is the transformation of another human being, then that desire will give way to facilitating hope in every circumstance. Act of influencing is the desire to give that influence away to help transform others. I think the unhealthy desire for success has become the new Mammon that Jesus warned about. He tells a bunch of people that they can only serve God or Mammon.[88]   Mammon was the North African God of wealth. Jesus was saying that we have to make a choice, either follow the oppressive, fruitless systems and faulty promises that you think you might find happiness in, or follow a God who offers something completely different. I wonder at this point in our journey as ones who follow in the way of Jesus, if we too have been following Mammon through the guise of success? It seems that we need to get out from underneath the tyranny of this kind of Christianity. Big Churches. Big Numbers. Big Billboards. These tend to get in the way of a movement. The problem is that most might agree with this assessment, but it doesn't seem like there is much in the way of change. I mean people like the idea of not being a big church but they still think it in the back of their heads, at least it seems that way with the language they use. I remember my first job here in the UK I worked as a Youth Pastor in a church and they told me during the interview that they were a church who didn't care about numbers, but when it came down to it, they did. They still used the language of success and failure when the church wasn't getting in enough converts. So maybe we need to get rid of the theology that makes it seem like conversion is anywhere in the Gospels. But if nothing changes, then the death of the Church is already imminent.

death.

If you ask someone who was around during the World Wars, they might tell you that the general attitude that pervaded society was that 'you just dealt with things'. Cultural historians call this period the Silent Generation because they weren't a very vocal culture. A lot of fundamental Christianity was effected by this period in our history. They were taught to simply accept things without challenge or question. Without the opportunity to dig deeper. It seems that the Christianity we have isn't willing to die to itself so that it can be resurrected. This is much more explicit than saying goodbye to dogma. Or even bigger than theology itself. This is about those who follow in the way of Jesus being willing to stand back and say when something is tragically wrong with what we are currently offering the world, being people who are willing to point it out. This isn't about reinvention. This is about death. Jesus uses death many times as an invitation to follow after Him[89]. This conspiracy of Jesus is about us coming to a place inside where we realize we need Him more than theology. More than what Calvin or Luther gave us. Although, without the history they have given us we wouldn't be able to start this conversation. This is a conversation, a dance - and God is the music. We need to start letting the music lead us rather than us trying to force the dance to fit the music. Maybe it's time to learn a new way to dance. It is about us living out this conspiracy dance together. So how do we do this practically? I think we start by coming to a place in our development as a Body of people who start to accept that this Jesus revolution begins with us asking questions. Deep in the fabric of every Jew was/is the reality that questioning is central to their development as individuals and as a people. When we read the story about Job, it is about a Jewish man being Jewish. He was asking questions. In our culture, this is defined as doubt. Maybe we've got our defintions wrong here. Maybe questioning wasn't ever the same about doubt. I think questions make it hard for us to comfortably keep our distance from truth. They challenge us to find out if what we believe is really worth believing. Most of us scared of this for good reason, it means we would have to change and let go of things. Maybe things that have been with us for most of our lives. Challenging age-old ideas and systems that have never had a place in our future. It is us going into our neighbourhoods and towns and asking what it looks like to be a people who invite "outsiders" into our conversation. This is where the change begins. This is where the conspiracy of Jesus starts. Most importantly, it starts with the death and letting go of the things we call home. This is what He's talking about when He challenges his followers in Luke 14:26 Jesus said, "if anyone comes to me and does not hate his father and mother, his wife and children, his brothers and sisters - yes, even his own life - he cannot be my disciple." Jesus gives us some insight into what He means through his choice of words. Towards the end of the verse, He turns from family connections and includes all of life in his challenge. This was the point of the verse. That to be a part of this movement that Jesus is introducing, we have to be willing to give up those things close to us, inside of us, that have somehow made a home within us. Those things we aren't willing to let go of are the very things we might have to abandon, even if it costs us our "life".

the word was.
In Matthew's letter, Chapter 18 verse 11, Jesus says why He came here which was to "seek and save the lost". Suppose humanity is like this beautiful fractured flower vase, but through the death of Jesus has come to be fixed - well then, either we are broken and not fixed, or we are fixed and not broken. If we are fixed and not

broken, then the life and death of Jesus becomes more about how we should be, not what we used to be. It doesn't mean we don't have the scar that we each carry, or that we will never make decisions that will hurt or marr those around us. It means we have the potential not to. if Jesus came to die for our sins, then it is all done. If we spend all of our time focusing on something that is destructive, then life does remain hopeless. But the message of Jesus was about hope, not about how bad we might be to the core of our being. If we so choose to follow this line of thinking, it would be like a doctor replacing our old bum leg and we respond by demanding our old leg over our new one. I hope we can come to a place where we realize that Jesus came here for more than saving us from our sin. Which is a dead issue.

Jesus says it this way, now watch his word choice: "The Son of Man came to seek and to save that which WAS lost[90]"... Through his own words, we can see that Jesus assumes that what he came to do has already been done. Or that has already been put into motion by just being with us. That his death and resurrection, but not just that, his being present with humanity is enough tol bring about a new identity. Not just for a few, but for all of mankind. The Aramaic word for lost is *abedah*. It means something that has been destroyed or is perishing. But it isn't dead just yet, there is still hope. The Son of Man wasn't a special title for Jesus, in fact, it was a title for anyone. In Aramaic it means 'man of the earth', when rendered correctly, it means 'I, anyone or someone'...it could mean any one of these three. It was a term of humility. Essentially Jesus is stating his mission statement from a place of humbled reverence for the lost, which in context were those who were concerned about their status. The "lost" wouldn't have been a general term, it would refer to those who have forgotten what it means to be a child. Those that have lost their innocence and wonder of life. Those who have let attempts at status drive them in all they say and do. Some might take this out of context and mean this verse to pertain to those are not in the 'Jesus Club', but if we take this all into context, then the lost become a very specific group of people, and even in this instance, it might even include those who follow him who have seemed to drop the ball[91].

Jesus might say something like this now: I am here to (or my aim is to) offer healing to those who have lost their innocence. Or "I exist to be a person who shows others what it means to redis-cover who God has meant them to be in light of these children that surround them."

In light of the WAS phrase another re-wording might sound like this: "I have humbly arrived in the here and now to fully heal those whose innocence has been destroyed…and teach them to rediscover what it looks like to be innocent once again…" This is a very different understanding of what most have taken this verse to mean. Having said that, it doesn't mean that Jesus didn't come for our redemption, it just means, in this verse here, He was talking about something a bit different than what we might usually hear. Which is that he invites us to surrender our ideas and find our innocence. Children are that reminder. This is another place where I think we don't take the message of Jesus far enough, because the phrase 'Son of Man' could mean anyone. It is a term of humiliated ambiguity. Jesus might not only be speaking of Himself here but also encouraging our potential along as well. That our responsibility is to formatively utilize things like social justice, meeting the needs of others, being fully present with someone, and loving without expectation to help redeem what seems to be lost. To walk into a situation that seems hopeless and be hope incarnate. To put flesh on what could be, rather than sitting back and hoping with the person in pain for something different, rather be the difference that could be.

Jesus was walking towards Jerusalem through the market towns of Samaria and Galilee and he's making his way through crowds and a series of conversations, when a young rich ruler (who some historians think could have been Saul of Tarsus) asks

Jesus what he needs to do to get in on what He's been talking about. Jesus goes through the conversation and lists off a few things and by the end of the story, the man walks off.

The man walks away.
Jesus doesn't chase after him.

He doesn't try to do some miracle to get his attention; Jesus doesn't use his divinity to get the guy to say a prayer. God's Son who came to the 'save the world', let's one of those He came to save walk right out the door. Jesus later tells the famous story about a teenage boy who runs in after school and asks for his inheritance. In the Jewish context, the son was basically saying to the father, "drop dead" and "I don't care if you starve". To ask for your inheritance while your father was alive was like giving your father the middle finger and embarrassing him and stomping on his public reputation. The father's neighbors who would have lived in an insular-type community would have easily caught wind of this "typical teenage behavior". In small Jewish communities, correcting one's child was done as a community rather than individually. It might have even included stoning the son. So what does the teenage boy do? He runs away. Who wouldn't?

But, the father doesn't chase the son.
He doesn't force his son back into the family either.

He waits in desperate anticipation and in the hope that one day the son might come to his senses and return. And as we all know, he does. What is even more interesting is that the father "was a long way off" when the son finally decided to come back. In the Aramaic, it would be like saying that there were miles and miles in between them. And yet, the father chases after the son, but only when the son chooses to return. This is also symbolic of what our actions have the potential to do when we are in relationship with one another.

Like create distance.
Hurt.
Pain.
Misunderstanding.
And broken hearts.

But still the father bridges the gap. The conspiracy of Jesus invites others to walk away and come back when and if they are ready. Fundamental evangelism says "we must get the sale!" Conspiracy evangelism says it is not our job to get the sale. The conspiracy invites us to an inner life with God. A life that relies upon God to take the lead. Or like Bono says, "...find out what God is doing and go join in on it!"

ernest shackleton.

Most people stay away from dark places. The tense stomach muscles and the dripping beads of sweat that accompany such a journey are enough to keep outdoor adventurer Ernest Shackleton away from the journey towards the inner life. Because it might just involve death. Giving up things. Saying goodbye to the past. Laying to rest the words of others and realizing that those words aren't the last word. We surround ourselves with so much noise that we drown out any possibility for us to hear the inner longings and pain that might be lurking in the caverns of our heart. Kat Kent, a Canadian psychotherapist says it this way, "A fear of closeness could develop into a person creating a 'false self'. A child who has been humiliated might grow up as a distant authoritative figure that nobody dares approach. Another person may hide his feeling of unworthiness by appearing loud and full of self-importance. The constant joker uses humour to keep a safe distance from those around him. The star whose success has depended on youth and beauty may not have learned how to develop relationships as a whole person."

All of us *are* broken.

Whether we know Jesus or not, we are a people fragmented and broken. Whatever we think we bring to the table, we bring it fragmented. It is in pieces, and it becomes less than it could be. I know Ii am contradicting myself here, because I have talked about how we are fixed, but it doesn't mean our wounds never rupture and or re-enter the atmosphere. We must be okay with apparent contradictions. It is the contradictions I think we need to talk about, but not necessarily change. Realizing that Jesus calls broken people to carry a broken message emancipates our inadequacies from a prison of perfection. The message isn't about how broken we are, it's about all that we can be and working together with one another and God to find what that looks like in every area of our lives. We need contradictions. Perfection itself is in process and so the way we become perfect is by being in process. The moment we stop, is the moment we stop becoming perfect. Shalom can rest in the arms of war. Not that war is a good thing. But these seemingly apparent contradictions weren't foreign to the ancient Hebrews. They embraced them as reality. They didn't run from them, they talked about them, they threw tantrums and wrote poetry about them. Their lives were lived in the constant awareness that contradictions weren't the enemy, but the fear of them is. I think it's a good thing when we come to a place where we don't try to fix the things that help us to grow. Contradictions can be benevolent to our existence. Running from them can be detrimental to that very same existence. Sociologist Freda Adler says this about the nature of contradictions, "That man is a creature who needs order yet yearns for change is the creative contradiction at the heart of the laws which structure his conformity and define his deviancy". Within the microcosm of our being is the realization that contradiction is our friend. Contradictions help shape us and our potential. The moment we run from our contradictions, the ones we get to taught to deny or aggressively ignore, is the same moment we begin to deny our humanity. There were some teenagers who caught onto this reality when the met Jesus.

teenage fisherman.

When Jesus met a few fumbling teenage fisherman on a shore miles from here, he knew who he was dealing with. Yet, he still chose them and their brokenness. We can't afford to see brokenness as a weakness any longer, but rather a requirement that God is looking for in all of his followers. David the poet king, invites us to see brokenness as something that draws us to the heart of God. David once wrote that "God is near the broken-hearted"[92]. Why? Because, we are a people who need distance from pain. Even though we know truth has the ability to heal, we have gotten used to not being whole. I would much rather have heard that my parents just couldn't take care of me, rather than find out that I was adopted because of their lifestyle of drugs. The young girl who runs away and becomes a prostitute would rather think her father died than that he left her because he just couldn't keep his commitments. We live in a world of broken promises, look around you and you will see what I'm talking about. Read your diary, you might even find the sting of betrayal throughout those pages. We live in our contexts afraid of connection, yet, we have pseudo-communities like Facebook and Myspace that make it seem otherwise. The ability to walk into what we fear and then walk out when it gets too close for us to handle is where safety and danger hold hands and we can go no further. The movement of Jesus invites us all into the places we have come to fear the most. Jesus himself enters into them with us and experiences the pain and healing alongside of us. He usually enters in with us through the presence of another. He is the one who offers to carry our burdens.

my old green duffel bag.

I have moved quite a bit in my life and I usually carry an old green duffel bag I got from the Navy. It was sort of the Linus' blanket for me without the cloud of dust. It went with me wherever I went. Whenever I entered my new home on my itinerant journey, I carried it with me. When Jesus invites us to come to him with all of our problems, worries, stresses and losses he offers to replace them with rest. In his words, he never says that those issues will be vaporised into some eternal abyss somewhere. He simply offers his rest. But his rest is something, even without knowing it, we might just crave. The word for rest that Jesus used in his everyday Aramaic was *Menuwchah*; it is the idea of consolation or comfort. If you dig deeper, you might even find more metaphors laced with romantic language. It would be like a lover saying "You can hide in me." or "I will catch your tears when they fall". There is something healing about the presence of God. This kind of language is drenching with metaphor that comes with a dozen roses and candle-light dinners. Jesus promises to be there with you.

He promises to experience it with you.

Let the realization that you will never be alone again permeate through every pore.You are not alone.The movement of Jesus reminds us we can't do this alone. It reminds us that we can't let others do this alone. It compels us to come to grips with the fact that accepting the truth of who we are and where we could be brings healing. The healing we receive is a gift that can't stop with us. It must be shared and given to others in need. There is something terribly divine in being with someone who is in the midst of experiencing loss. Here's the challenge, find someone to be with - or maybe you need to find someone to be there for you.

The Anatomy of a Movement

Not all who wander are lost – Tolkien

Believe nothing on the faith of traditions,
even though they have been held in honor
for many generations and in diverse places.
Do not believe a thing because many people speak of it.
Do not believe on the faith of the sages of the past.
Do not believe what you yourself have imagined,
persuading yourself that a God inspires you.
Believe nothing on the sole authority of your masters and priests.
After examination, believe what you yourself have tested
and found to be reasonable, and conform your conduct thereto.
Buddha

God wants to write a good story with you. God is still writing the ancient words of scripture. But, now the pages are your life and the black and the white are the choices that you make. He believes you have what it takes. He is there with you every step of the way. The journey begins in darkness. The unknown. It doesn't end there, it starts in the places we have known too well. We are invited to do some spring cleaning of the soul, an emptying of ourselves for the sake of the world. We live in a post-enlightenment society that has created a hunger for knowledge at the expense of truth. The Church itself has colluded with this post-enlightenment approach to gnosis. If we search through the annals of the Church mystics and the mystics of many other religions we will see a common thread of men and women who were more than okay with the tension of living in darkness[93]. The unknown author of *The Cloud of Uknowing* comments on our need for mischevious wonder, "The most Godlike knowledge of God is that which is known by

165

unknowing'. If we are all honest we can agree that we have culti-vated a fear of the unknown.There are many fears in our world, and this seems to be the most prominent one that follows us into shadows. Out of this fear, we have created mirages of truth, where we think what we have quenches the thirst we have longed for since birth. Some of these mirages are things like doctrine[94], absolute truth, exclusivism, rhetoric and consumerism to name a few. Places like Disneyworld and television commercials invite us into a world where consumerism paints a "whole new world[95]" of possibilities and how the commodification process is a necessary companion to have when we try to understand the things we are chasing after. In his book "Vinyl Leaves, Walt Disney World and America", Stephen M. Fjellman analyses Disney World and how it incarnates a (post-modern[96]) society based on consumerism. (He also says this): Disney is a major corporation that has a vested interest in promoting a consumerist society. Disney World is not merely a collection of fantasies for children, it is actively advocating the utopia of happy consumerism. "Our lives can only be well lived (or lived at all) through the purchase of commodities. As the commodity form becomes a central part of culture, so culture becomes available for use in the interest of commodification, as a legitimation for the entire system. We must be taught that it is good, reasonable, just, and natural that the means necessary for life are available only through the market". In this context, here is how Disney world is defined: "Walt Disney World produces, packages and sells experiences and memories as commodities." Visitors know that when going in Disney World, they get into a place where all their activities are controlled and conditioned (e.g. queues, sound-tracks all over the parks, visual magnets like the Cinderella castle) . They know that their experiences and souvenirs will be manufactured and probably not so different from the ones of another visitor. But they still buy the package because they know they will get a very enjoyable experience." This spirit of commodification has now moved the church into an industry of marketing certain aspects of Christianity. It has also created a pervasive dynamic where people want to know what they are buying into rather than being okay with the intrigue of mystery that the eastern followers of God found so hauntingly comfortable. These Disney-Church adherents crave the ability to know every detail of every iota of truth. Rather than allow truth to be truth by itself, we thwart its very nature. This makes life more dangerous when we let truth and uncertainty be themselves. Life becomes more risky. More open to possibilities. Jesus did not intend to start some organization that met together a few times a week. He started a movement. There is a reason why the Apostle Paul calls it a body, because a body moves. It is about progression. Forward motion.

A movement for anyone.
Sociologists typically define social movements in four categories[97]: Alternative social movements, Reformative social movements, Redemptive social movements and Revolutionary social movements. For example, Reformative movements predominantly spend a lot of their energy mostly trying to change laws. I think its crucial to remember that movements happen in groups. Even if a movement starts with one person, it never ever ends with just one. The nature of any movement is that it grows and evolves. Once a movement gains momentum it is an unstoppable force[98] to be reckoned with. The Church might be better off as a movement.

A movement is not an institution. When Martin Luther King Jr. started the movement toward equality, his vision wasn't a large building that gathered people together to talk about peace and togetherness, it was a dream built upon a possible reality that involved real people doing substantially transformational things. He shared his vision because it depended on humanity, not just Christians working together. It was a dream that involved active participation. This is the kind of movement Jesus invites anyone and everyone to get on board with.

It is a movement of art enthusiasts, not art critics. If you ever listen to any critic for that matter, they spend a lot of energy telling you what's wrong with the painting or work of art; they never really express how beautiful the contours of the work are. They will tell you why they think it has no value. Or why the quality of the paint doesn't do justice to the painting. And the list goes on. But, if you have ever met an art enthusiast you might see why the world can be beautiful again. They believe anything is possible. That green could possibly go with purple, and contrasting colors like fuschia could shine alongside a golden tree. Their world is filled with what ifs rather than "no, we can't do this because..." And they are even willing to break the mold a bit. They are willing to break the handbook on what not to do to make sure the message within the art gets out. They will create new genres of art, they will build links with the heretics and outsiders who continue to challenge the way art is seen by the world. Those in the movement aren't afraid of these kinds of contributors, in fact, those that are in the movement invite them in because they need them to keep moving. We all need to relearn the art of being an enthusiast for forward motion. The danger is that we become a movement that never moves. We become stale and petrified by all the what ifs rather than excited about what is around the bend.

A movement is leaderless. Because everyone leads in some way or another. When you go to work and treat the office nerd like a regular human being, you have already led in a way that no one else could have. And without knowing it, you have changed a system, one moment of grace at a time. It doesn't mean that the movement won't ever have those that inspire or those that chastise or those who rethink everything. It means that no one person is vying for the leadership role because there isn't one to fight over. The Apostle Paul once said this: "And we know that in all things God works together for the good of those who love him, who have been called according to his purpose[99]." Many people have intepreted this verse in such a way that God has pre-chosen people to be a part of his exclusive club that has certain membership benefits that include salvation from a fiery pit. Yet if we revisit this verse in its context, the message might be a bit different and even highly demonstrative of what a movement could look like. Paul was dealing with a lot in the church of Rome. "Ancient Rome boasted hundreds of pagan temples. Paul wrote his letter to the Romans from the rowdy port city of Corinth, where sexual immorality and prostitution were openly practiced. Yet Rome was even more idolatrous than Corinth. Sporting events in the Circus Maximus[100] and fertility Goddess worship in pagan temples echoed the adulation of idolatrous Romans. Rome was a city wholly given to idolatry"[101]. So Paul is dealing with a people group who are learning to let go of some bad habits. What are your bad habits? We all have them, some we aren't even aware of. And Paul is playing on the word love here, some of the readers would have heard love as sex which would have implied prostitution, but Paul is redefining their take on love and challenging them to see everything through the lens of this new kind of love that God can show them. There is more to his message than this though. The word 'called' that Paul uses in the Greek means 'to invite'. Sometimes we hear the word call and think it means that all people are 'called' into a specific task of some sort to complete while they are here on earth. History has shown that the 'idea of calling' as we know it came from Martin Luther, not Paul, Jesus or any other biblical writer. Not to say we don't each have a purpose, but it is not found in theological equations. The invitation or 'calling' that Paul is talking about is open to everyone, not just a specific few. The grammatical tense of the word is inclusive of masses not a single group of people. The Greek word *synergeō* means "to work together", it is a synergy or partnership of things working together for a common goal. God is inviting anyone and everyone to partner with Him. The word for purpose was the same word for the type of bread called showbread[102] which was used in a Jewish temple practice and put on display for everyone to see. It is a public experience, one that the whole community gets to share in. This verse is less about who gets in the club of Christian and more about inviting all kinds of new creative collaborators to join the movement. A movement is open for anyone who wants to be a part. Anyone.

The movement of Jesus is redemptive, not judgemental. It doesn't change things by pointing the finger, it changes things by loving people. It is a movement that is reformational, revolutionary and at times can be counter-intuitive to the culture of the world and the culture of the Church. This new kind of movement is one that has the ability to leave the adverse effects of structural functionalism or fundamentalism behind and pave new horizons for the Church to come. There is hope for those who say they follow Jesus. But the hope of Jesus never stopped with those who followed Him. It was meant to be a public movement of people who did and said things in such a way that those they came into contact with (including one another) would be so curious about the counter-cultural revolution that they might want to join in that moment. And our response should be one of open-arms. No matter what their background or lifestyle choice is or was. Love is the movement. I wonder what it would look like if the Church decided to truly love. When I say love, I mean the unfiltered kind. The greatest kind of love in the Greek is *agape*. It is loosely translated as the ability to love someone and do things for the benefit of that person without expecting anything in return —- ever. If we love people with the expectation of them changing, than that is called filtered love, it comes with the hope of something in return – their transformation. Love unfiltered steps on the scene and simply accepts a person as they are without ulterior motives. Love believes its about the other and not ourselves. It believes its

Off
Off
Off
Off
Off
Off
Off
Off
Off
Off
Off
Off
Off
Off
Off

not about theology, but the person. This is an integral part to the message of Jesus.

a want ad.

There is a want ad posted in the classifieds of life waiting for you to respond to it. The open opportunity sounds something like this: "The Rabbi Jesus is looking for people who want to affect societies, economies, political systems, ecosystems, religious systems, belief systems and hearts. He is looking for men, women, children, homosexuals, Baptists, Buddhists, Mormons, terrorists, young, old, blind, crippled, amoral people, and atheists who want to be a part of movement to restore heaven on earth. To pronounce a new way of life is bursting forth on the scene and that this new way of life is one where we all get to make things right: promote justice, love the unlovable, embrace the lost son, find truth in obscure corners and learn what it means to follow after a Rabbi who believes everyone has what it takes." By the way, the position hasn't been filled yet, it's waiting for you on the other side of this page – just turn the page.

Notes

[1] This chapter is going to set the scene and put some terms we might have become comfortable with back in their original context and find out what they mean and why they are important to us today. If you already familiar with these, please read on.

[2] Aramaic was the typical speaking language of Jesus, Hebrew is the modernized version

[3] This statement seems to say that I know what the exact message of Jesus would be, this book is not about projecting a "right way" to see things attitude, it is just adding to the conversation that has been going on within the Christian community.

[4] http://www.newadvent.org/cathen/02369a.htm

[5] http://www.answers.com/topic/mosaic-law#cite_note-0

[6] The Kingdom or the Kingdom of God is a phrase Jesus tends to use and might be better rendered as a "way of life"

[7] i wonder what kind of policies we have in our governments/churches that do the same?

[8] There is historical/scholarly evidence that supposes Judas' last name iscariot might be a misspelling. Which changes our story and thoughts on Judas just a little. Maybe he wasn't the villain we make him out to be.

[9] (By the way, i think Judas gets a bad rap here. He thought Jesus was coming to overthrow Rome, so Judas was setting the stage for Jesus to come in and take over the emperor's spot. We see Judas dripping in guilt and throwing the 'blood money' back into the lap of the Pharisees because he gave up on Jesus being the Messiah when Jesus chose not to fight *back*.)

[10] http://www.copingskills4kids.net/thinking-coping-brain

[11] Just a quick note, the Pharisees aren't the bad guys, they're

in the story to remind us that we too can easily follow down the path of turning scripture into a dogmatic plumbline. They had good intentions, but is that good enough?

12 Matthew 5

13 Read Jesus Wants To Save Christians by Rob Bell.

14 This would be like telling someone today that they are a diamond or block of gold. Something that holds immense value and can sway opinions and systems.

15 1 Peter 3:18 (NiV)

16 I think if we're not careful, we too can join in his "pre-conversion" crusade in the name of protecting our versions of truth.

17 Acts 9

18 2 Cor. 5:17 (TNiV)

19 These are tracts or pamphlets handed out with a "plan for salvation". Which tends to include a prayer at the end that people can ask for forgiveness and ask Jesus into their lives. This isn't wrong or invaluable, it might be a bit anemic though.

20 Isaiah 55:9 (NiV)

21 John 4:34

22 For some this way of thinking is 'old hat', its good to be reminded, just in case we slip back into old habits...

23 http://en.wikipedia.org/wiki/Metanarrative

24 Be on the lookout for my next book on understanding the terminology in Christianity we have become accustomed to. 'Colloquial Christianity: Finding God After Theology' - out soon!

25 http://wiki.ikon.org.uk/wiki/index.php/Main_Page

26 Matthew 19:18-20 (my translation)

27 http://www.csulb.edu/~eruyle/ecumen/with%20marx %20&%20jesus.htm

28 Be on the lookout for my new initiative that seeks to invite all religious people and people from all backgrounds to join in on

dialogue that

29 Crow and Weasel by Barry Lopez

30 In a sermon at Mars Hill Church – www.marshill.org

31 Matthew 18:21-22 (NIV)

32 Google: Bear Flag Revolt

33 Luke 19:46 (NLT)

34 Luke 5:17-26 (NIV)

35 www.absoluteastronomy.com/topics/Tree_of_
Knowledge_of_Good_and_Evil

36 Ecclesiastes 3:11 (NIV)

37 John 8:1-11

38 Hebrews 10:10

39 A great article on this at: www.pomomusings.com

40 I personally do not see an 'us and them' mentality; the idea that homosexuality is a sin has been hijacked by bad hermeneutics. I see homosexuality as simply another way of life we call learn from.

41 http://www.trainingforchange.org/matt_guynn

42 John 10:30 (NIV)

43 Thanks to Rob Bell for this distinction; Velvet Elvis by Rob Bell

44 *21:1-22:5(NIV)*

45 This philosophy tends to get used in atheist circles,; I am reframing this word as an explanation of how useless words are in explaining God, and how that reality draws us deeper into the mystery that is God rather than groping through theology.

46 http://biblestudy2000.tripod.com/Biblestudy2000a/id1.html

47 I think The West needs to be revisiting these questions, for the sanctity of human life is at stake.

48 Most churches spend a lot of time deciphering what Christ is talking about here and tend to use cryptic language and ethereal descriptions of what it all might mean. They say things like "...it means that we have to give up everything

we want" or "let go of all of our dreams". This is not the case at all.

49   I am not codoning religious suicide or tribal murder. I am simply using the same imagery Jesus did as a metaphor for passion and direction.

50   Thanks to Rob Bell for this insight. www.marshill.org

51   http://www.jewishanswers.org/ask-the-rabbi-2566/the-jewish-view-of-satan/

52   Most people hear the word 'darkness' and think pervasive actions or destructive choices, but there is something deeper in the Hebrew language that is going on, darkness can also be a synonym for developmental conflict.

53   Again, it's good to remember that I am not saying that there isn't good or bad, but that love is the ultimate reality. Love is the most important. Love has the last word, not whether something is good or bad.

54   The sefirot are the ten archetypal attributes or characteristics of the Godhead – within Jewish mysticism.

55   http://en.allexperts.com/q/Conservative-Judaism-951/2008/8/purpose-animal-sacrifices.htm

56   Ecclesiastes 3:1 (NIV)

57   http://www.tikkun.org/article.php/Rose-Divinegarb

58   John 5:19 (NIV)

59   1 Corinthians 9:22 (NIV)

60   When I refer to things being human, this isn't the same as saying 'sinful', sometimes within certain christian circles, the word gets used synonmously. This is the case for most of what is written here. Also, Jesus did approach the world with a non-dualistic approach, but usually challenged those who saw the world dualistically.

61   http://www.gnosis.org/naghamm/gop.html

62   1 Corinthians 3:9 (ISV)

63   http://dictionary.reference.com/browse/synergy

64   A metaphor for heaven. Although the theology of heaven is

currently being rediscovered as a possible metaphor for enlightenment or that God dwells here. Heaven is here, not there.

65 (when I used the word myth, I don't mean lies or fables, I mean the powerful narrative that is deeply embedded within our society and history — that carries us along, and something we get to add to)

66 Psalm 130:5 (NIV)

67 http://en.wikipedia.org/wiki/Heuristic

68 http://en.wikipedia.org/wiki/Black_swan_theory

69 (I would say 5% of the time; I am being generous because I am writing the book and not my wife!)

70 http://www.mts.net/~baumel/

71 Luke 15

72 I used Greek here to show that even in the Bible we have now, the idea of sin wasn't epidemic

73 This book isn't about rehashing our history, but it is a mirror into how maybe our misinterpretations have given us a history that we may need to seek peace and healing for, such as the Crusades to name one example.

74 Lord of the Rings by J.R.R. Tolkien

75 Genesis 12:1-3 (Amplified Bible)

76 The Baal Shem Tov is a title of a renowned Rabbi named Yisrael Ben Eliezer who lived in the 1600-1700's. The title means "The Master of the Good Name". Find out more here: http://www.baalshemtov.com/whowashe.htm

77 This was the Rabbi who succeeded the Baal Shem Tov. Find out more: http://www.berdichev.org/the_passing_of_the _maggid.htm

78 It was a work dissecting the meaning of Alice in Wonderland.

79 Genesis 1:1

80 Now, there are many good writers and books that have tried to dissect how the Trinity works, and i am not going to do it

here and i think it is also good to know there are things we aren't going to know and that's okay. And also never to stop asking questions, it essential to our journey. Jewish thought contends that God is one not three.

81 www.aish.com search 'Shema Prayer'

82 Genesis Chapters 16-19

83   Google: Paleolithic History

84 John 17:13

85 Genesis 17:5

86 Deuteronomy 9:23

87 I am purposefully taking this verse out of context to prove a point about how consumerism has snuck in and hijacked the context from us.

88 Matthew 6:19-24

89 Mark 8:34

90 Note: There are scholarly disputes (and you might see this in some different bible versions; for example, this verse doesn't show up in the New Living Translation but will in the KJV))

91 The Hebrew word for 'seek' is baqash, which means 'aim' and the word save in the Hebrew means 'to heal'

92 Psalm 34:18 (NRSV)

93 When I use the word darkness in this context, it means the unknown. it does not signify ignorance in any sense of the word.

94 (Which is different from absolute certainty; and this is the line where most people part ways because the lack of distinction and terminology)

95 Thanks to Disney's Aladdin for this little ditty.

96 I would disagree with the post-modern assertion only because the creation of disney products has been around long before the conversation of post-modernism was.

97 http://en.wikipedia.org/wiki/Social_movement#Types_of_social_movement

98 Thanks to Erwin Mcmanus for this phrase. Check out his

book by the same name.

99   Romans 8:28 (NiV)

100 http://en.wikipedia.org/wiki/Circus_ Maximus

101 http://www.gaychristian101.com/Romans-1.html

102 http://en.wikipedia.org/wiki/Shewbread

BOOKS

O is a symbol of the world, of oneness and unity. In different cultures it also means the "eye," symbolizing knowledge and insight. We aim to publish books that are accessible, constructive and that challenge accepted opinion, both that of academia and the "moral majority."

Our books are available in all good English language bookstores worldwide. If you don't see the book on the shelves ask the bookstore to order it for you, quoting the ISBN number and title. Alternatively you can order online (all major online retail sites carry our titles) or contact the distributor in the relevant country, listed on the copyright page.

See our website www.o-books.net for a full list of over 500 titles, growing by 100 a year.

And tune in to myspiritradio.com for our book review radio show, hosted by June-Elleni Laine, where you can listen to the authors discussing their books.

MySpiritRadio